Islam and Mental Health

Beliefs, Research and Applications

Harold G. Koenig, M.D.
Duke University Medical Center and
King Abdulaziz University Faculty of Medicine

Saad Saleh Al Shohaib, M.D.
King Abdulaziz University Faculty of Medicine and
Bagedo and Erfan Hospital

Copyright © 2017 Harold G. Koenig

All rights reserved.

ISBN-13: 978-1544730332
ISBN-10: 1544730330

DEDICATION

To our wives, Charmin and Hosah

CONTENTS

	Introduction	1
1	Mental Health of Muslims	2
2	Historical Background	5
3	Core Islamic Beliefs	8
4	Islamic Practices	15
5	Islamic Values	19
6	Islam and Mental Health: Speculations	26
7	Islam and Mental Health: The Research	38
8	Clinical Applications	50
9	Overcoming Barriers to Mental Health Care	61
10	Summary and Conclusions	64
	References	66
	About the Authors	78

INTRODUCTION

With 1.6 billion adherents, Islam is the second largest religion making up 23.4% of the world's population in 2010 (Pew Research Center, 2011). Based on current birth rates, Islam is projected to increase to 29.7% of the world's population in 2050, to 32.3% in 2070 (equaling the percentage Christian), and to 34.9% by 2100 (exceeding the percentage of Christians, which at that time will be 33.8%) (Pew Research Center, 2015). This makes Islam the world's fastest growing religion, increasing at a rate of 1.5% per year (double that of non-Muslims). Less than one quarter of the world's Muslim population lives in the Middle East and Northern Africa, whereas nearly two-thirds live in the Asia-Pacific region (particularly Indonesia, Malaysia, India, Pakistan, and Bangladesh). Only 0.3% of Muslims live in the Americas, although this amounts to over 5 million people, a number expected to exceed 10 million by 2030.

In this small book, we examine the prevalence of mental disorder among Muslims, briefly review the historical development of Islam, and then concisely describe Islamic beliefs, practices, and values. Based on those, we speculate on the relationship between religion and mental health in Muslims, hypothesizing both positive and negative effects that Islam may have on mental health. This is then followed by a systematic review of quantitative research on religiosity and mental health in Muslims (along with a comparison of mental health in Muslims and non-Muslims) in order to put those speculations to the test. Original research from worldwide datasets is presented here for the first time. Finally, we make suggestions for mental health professionals on how to apply these research findings to clinical practice when treating Muslim clients. Each chapter ends with an easy to read summary of take-home points ("conclusions").

The **primary audience** for this book is mental health professionals and clergy who are called upon to help Muslims deal with emotional and other mental health problems. However, given the careful attention to documentation, emphasis on research, and report of original research results, investigators who conduct studies in Muslim populations, as well as healthcare systems that provide services to Muslim patients, will also find this volume useful. Finally, lay Muslims more generally will discover that the information contained here may be both enlightening and faith enhancing.

CHAPTER 1

MENTAL HEALTH OF MUSLIMS

Religion and mental health are very sensitive issues in the Arab world and Islam today. Many Muslims feel targeted by others, which no doubt has consequences on their mental health and well-being. At every point in this book we seek to objectively and even-handedly present and discuss these sensitive topics which psychiatrists, therapists, and pastoral counselors need to know about when treating Muslims. We believe that religious beliefs and practices can bring tremendous solace and hope, but the misunderstanding of or distortion of those beliefs can also lead to much pain and distress.

Despite the potential buffering effects of devout religious faith, mental health problems are not uncommon among Muslims. Rates of significant depressive symptoms in American Muslims range from 27.9% to 61.9% depending on method of assessment and population studied (Hodge et al., 2015; Amer & Hovey, 2012; Abu-Ras & Abu-Bader, 2009). Similarly, significant anxiety symptoms are present in 24.9% to 65.4% of American Muslims (Amer & Hovey, 2012; Abu-Ras & Abu-Bader, 2009). Emotional disorders are also prevalent in Muslims outside the United States (U.S.), although there is little research examining mental disorders specifically in Muslims. In one of the few such studies, the rate of mood disorders diagnosed using the WHO CIDI in 366 adult Muslims in southern Ethiopia was

15.3% (Awas et al., 1999), compared to 9.6% in the general population of the U.S. (Demyttenaere et al., 2004). Of course, this comparison is between Ethiopia and the U.S., and does not account the socioeconomic and environment differences between the U.S. and this poverty-stricken African country.

Rates of mental disorder in Muslim-majority countries (rather than in Muslims specifically) are more readily available. For example, the rates of depression and anxiety disorders in 766 adults living in rural Bangladesh (a country which is over 80% Muslims) was 8.0% and 5.0%, respectively, based on examination by a psychiatrist using DSM-IV diagnostic criteria (Hosain et al., 2007). In a study of 1,475 adults attending Primary Health Care Centers in Qatar (nearly 70% Muslim), rates of psychiatric disorder identified using the WHO CIDI diagnostic interview were 18.3% for major depression, 17.3% for any anxiety disorder, 14.1% for personality disorder, 6.6% for psychosis, and 0.8-1.4% for substance use disorder (Bener et al., 2015).

Finally, using DSM-IV-R and ICD-10 criteria, the 2010 Global Burden of Disease (GBD) Study found that major depressive disorder contributed only a small percentage (2.6-4.0%) to overall disability-adjusted life-years (DALYs) among adults in 22 Arab countries (Algeria, Egypt, Bahrain, Comoros, Djibouti, Iraq, Jordan, Saudi Arabia, Kuwait, Lebanon, Libya, Mauritania, Morocco, Oman, Palestinian territory, Qatar, Yemen, Somalia, Sudan, Syria, Tunisia, United Arab Emirates) (Mokdad et al., 2014). On the other hand, the GBD Study also found that DALYs from mental disorders overall were higher in North Africa and the Middle East than in other regions in the world (Whiteford et al., 2015). The prevalence of mental disorders among children and adolescents has been estimated to be 12.8% in the Middle East compared to 12.0% in Europe and 19.9% in North America (Polanczyk et al., 2015).

Conclusions
Mental disorders and emotional problems are common among Muslims living in and outside the U.S. The reasons for this are numerous. Many Muslims outside of the U.S. live in poverty and in socioeconomically deprived areas of the world affected by war and terrorism. Those living in the U.S. or other western countries are in a different cultural environment where there is often internal conflict

between their Islamic values and the surrounding community (especially among young Muslims). In addition, Muslims are likely to experience discrimination in western countries, where they may have difficulty finding employment, be excluded from social or community groups, or even fearful of their safety (targeted for their religious beliefs or dress).

Thus, mental health professionals are likely to encounter Muslim clients in their practices and therefore need to know something about how Islam developed historically, what Muslim believe and practice today, and how these beliefs and practices are related to mental health.

CHAPTER 2

HISTORICAL BACKGROUND

Islam and Muslim both come from the same Arabic verb "s-l-m", which means to submit or surrender. "Islam" means the act of submitting to God's will, whereas "Muslim" identifies the person who submits. This religion, along with Judaism and Christianity, claims a tradition that dates back to Abraham, the father of the great monotheistic tradition who is thought to have lived somewhere between 2100 and 1600 BCE (McClellan, 2012). Islam is strictly monotheistic -- belief in one God (Allah). It arose in the 7th century CE out of the polytheistic Bedouin culture of the Arabian peninsula in the region of Mecca. Mecca is located in western Saudi Arabia about 40 miles inland from the Red Sea. In 610 CE, the Prophet Muhammad at the age of 40 is believed to have received his first revelation from the angel Gabriel in a cave on mount Hira during a time of deep prayer. These revelations continued intermittently over the next 22 years until his death in 632 CE. Since the Prophet Muhammad could not read or write, the angel Gabriel urged him to share his revelations with his companions, who carefully documented them on stone tablets, bones, and date palm leaves. These were eventually brought together into a single text (the Holy Qur'an) that was canonized around 653-656 CE by the third caliph, Uthman ibn Affan. The Arabic script in which the present day Qur'an is written (*scripta plena*) was not fully perfected until the middle of the 9th century (Esack, 2005).

Muslims believe that the Qur'an confirms many of the earlier Biblical scriptures that came before it (Qur'an 5:48). However, those scriptures contained errors, requiring that God reveal this final scripture (39:1-2). Muslims believe that the Prophet Muhammad was not inspired by God, but was rather a vessel through which God directly transmitted his word to humanity (word for word and without error). In fact, attributing the content of the Qur'an to the Prophet Muhammad is considered to be blasphemous in Islam. Muslims believe that the Qur'an supersedes all previous scriptures and represents God's final word from now until the end of time: "We sent to you [Muhammad] the Scripture with the truth, confirming the scriptures that came before it, and with *final authority* over them…" (5:48).[1]

By the end of the Prophet's life, Islam had spread throughout most of Arabia. During the 30 years after his death, it would spread through war and conquest far beyond the Arabian peninsula. Within 100 years it reached as far west as Spain, as far north and east as China and central Asia, and as far south as North Africa. Along with spread of the religion came Islamic law (*shari'ah*) and the many health-related beliefs and practices associated with it. Islamic law was then as it is today based on the Qur'an, the sayings and traditions of the Prophet (Hadith), and the practices of the early Muslim community (Sunnah) recorded in the early 8th century by Islamic scholars called "traditionalists." Four schools of Islamic law arose by the end of the 11th century: the Hanafi, the Maliki, the Shafi, and the Hanbali (the latter being more conservative in its interpretation). Wahhabi is a small branch off the Hanbali school and considered the most conservative of all Sunni groups.

Around the year 661 CE, war erupted in Iraq-Arabia over who would succeed Muhammad as caliph (or leader) of the Muslim world, causing a split between Sunni and Shia Muslims, one that remains to this day. In the 13th century, Sufi Muslims (a mystical branch of

---

[1] From here on, unless otherwise noted, all quotations from the Qur'an are from the translation by M.A.S. Abdel Haleem (*The Qur'an*, Oxford World's Classics, NY, NY: Oxford University Press, 2004)

Islam that focuses on purification of the inner self and connecting with God) split off from the Sunni branch. These splits have produced three major groups of Muslims: Sunni, Shia, and Sufi. Most Muslims today are Sunni (85%), followed by Shia (10-13%) and Sufi. Shia Muslims reside primarily in Iran, Iraq, Pakistan, and Lebanon. The percentage of Muslims who are Sufi is unknown, but Sufis can be either Sunni or Shia, and most currently reside in Turkey and other countries in South Asia and sub-Saharan Africa. Many Muslims may not consider themselves members of any of these three branches, according to the Pew Research Center (2012), which found approximately 20% of Muslims indicating that they were simply "Just a Muslim." Most of the conflict today in the Muslim world is between Sunnis (represented by Saudi Arabia) and Shia (represented by Iran).

Conclusions

This brief history provides an important background that will help the reader appreciate the source of Islamic beliefs and practices, the spread of Islam throughout the Middle East, Southern and Southeast Asia, and Africa, and the divisions in the Muslim world today.

CHAPTER 3

CORE ISLAMIC BELIEFS

In order to understand the relationship between Islam and mental health, it is important to know what Muslims believe, the religious practices that characterize day-to-day life, and the values and morals rooted in those beliefs and practices. Islamic beliefs and practices are integrated into all aspects of society, government, and the law in some areas of the world, particularly in the Middle East and North Africa.

Action or behavior is more important than belief in religions such as Buddhism, Hinduism, and perhaps Judaism. Not so in Islam. Having correct belief is very important in this religion. The most important beliefs are summarized in the confession of faith that Muslims testify to when converting to Islam (the Shahada): "La ilaha illa Allah, Muhammad rasoolu Allah" ("There is no true god but God, and Muhammad is the Messenger of God"). This statement emphasizes the oneness of God (called *tawhid*) and that Muhammad is God's messenger and final prophet.

Islam is grounded on six beliefs:
1. Belief in God
2. Belief in the Prophets
3. Belief in Divine Books
4. Belief in the Day of Judgement
5. Belief in Angels
6. Belief in Destiny

Belief in God

Muslims believe that Allah (literally, "the God") is the direct source of all Islamic teachings in the Qur'an. God is considered the creator of everything that exists and sustains all that exists. God is infinitely wise and tremendously forgiving, but also serves as judge and his punishment can be severe (3:12). God sees everything humans do, hears everything that people say, and controls everything that occurs in the universe. Nothing happens against God's will (9:51). People have freedom of choice, and can decide either to do things according to God's will or against it. Acting against God's will, says the Qur'an, will have severe consequences (see 2:39, 2:81, 2:174, and many more).

Contemporary Muslim theologian Fazlur Rahman (1998) says the attributes of God that relate to humans are "creation, sustenance, guidance, and judgement." With sustenance comes God's mercy and love, which is emphasized throughout the Qur'an. Indeed, the first verse of the Qur'an (1:1) is "In the name of God, the Lord of Mercy, the Giver of Mercy!" This verse is repeated at the start of every one of the 114 chapters contained in the Qur'an (except the 9th chapter). Another translation of 1:1 is: "In the Name of Allah, the Most Gracious, the Most Merciful" (Al-Hilali & Khan, 1996). The verse in Arabic is "Bismi Allāhi Ar-Rahmāni Ar-Rahīmi" (بِسْمِ اللهِ الرَّحْمنِ الرَّحِيم). Muslims believe that God is just, fair, forgiving, and especially *merciful* (but only to those who submit their lives to him).

Belief in the Prophets

Muslims believe that a prophet is a "messenger" through whom God reveals his word to humanity for its good. Islamic theologian Seyyed Hossein Nasr (2002, p 17) says that "revelation" is the direct conveying of a message from heaven that comes to prophets alone, and is distinguished from "inspiration," which is available to all people. The prophets in Islam began with Adam and from there have included Noah, Abraham, Ishmael, Jacob, Moses, David, Elijah, John the Baptist, and Jesus the Christ (*Isa al-Mesiah*). Jesus is highly revered (as is his mother Mary) (2:253; 3:55; 5:46). Jesus is considered the only prophet to have been raised up to heaven by God himself (3:55). However, Muslims believe that he did not die on the cross for people's sins (4:157) and is not God (as Christians believe) (5:17). Muslims believe that Jesus was the last prophet before the coming of the final prophet, the Prophet Muhammad.

During the time when the Prophet Muhammad began receiving revelations, those in Arabia worshiped many different gods, angels, the sun, moon, and a wide range of idols. Central to these revelations was that there is only one God and that all people are to submit their lives to God. Muslims do not worship the Prophet Muhammad, as Christians worship Jesus Christ, but rather consider him to be an exemplar whose life and deeds are to be emulated. Only God is to be worshiped, though, not Muhammad. Worshiping anyone but God is called "shirk" (associating "partners" with God). Shirk is considered the gravest of all sins in Islam, and is the only sin that God will not forgive unless a person is pardoned before death: "God does not forgive the joining of partners with Him: anything less than that He forgives to whoever He will, but anyone who joins partners with God has concocted a tremendous sin" (4:48).

Belief in Divine Books
In the Introduction of the Oxford World's Classics edition of *The Qur'an* (perhaps the best and most easily read English translation of the Qur'an to date), M.A.S. Abdel Haleem (2004) writes:

> "The Qur'an was the starting point for all the Islamic sciences. Arabic grammar was developed to serve the Qur'an, the study of Arabic phonetics was pursued in order to determine the exact pronunciation of Qur'anic words, the science of Arabic rhetoric was developed in order to describe the features of the inimitable style of the Qur'an, the art of Arabic calligraphy was cultivated through writing down the Qur'an, the Qur'an is the basis of Islamic law and theology; indeed, as the celebrated fifteenth-century scholar and author Suyuti said, 'Everything is based on the Qur'an.' The entire religious life of the Muslim world is built around the text of the Qur'an" (p ix).

Muslims believe that the Qur'an is the infallible Word of God, dictated directly to the Prophet Muhammad by the angel Gabriel reading from the original "mother book" in Heaven. As a result, members of all branches of Islam revere this holy book and follow its teachings. The Qur'an consists of 114 chapters (called *suras*) with numbered verses (*ayas*). Other sources of Islamic teaching (but not considered infallible like the Qur'an) are the Hadith (sayings of the Prophet) and the Sunnah (religious practices established by the Prophet that describe how the Prophet and followers lived). In the Sunni branch of Islam, there are six primary collections of Hadith: Sahih Bukhari, Sahih Muslim, Sunan Abu Dawood, Sunan al-Sughra, Jami at-Tirmidhi, and Sunan ibn Majah. Sahih Bukhari and Sahih Muslim are considered the most dependable in terms of reporting what the Prophet said. Among Shia Muslims, there are four major Hadith collections: the Kitab al-Kafi, Man la yahduruhu al-Fqih, Tahdhib al-Ahkam, and Al-Istibsar. Differences between Sunni and Shia Hadith are primarily based on scholars' opinions regarding the reliability of early companions of the Prophet who reported his sayings. Muhammad al-Bukhari (Sahih Bukhari) is believed to be the most reliable source of Sunni Hadith.

Muslims also recognize three books (or sets of books) from the Bible: the Torah (Genesis, Exodus, Leviticus, Numbers, and Deuteronomy), the Psalms, and the Gospels. With regard to the Gospels, Muslims believe that the original Gospels were revealed by God to Jesus, who himself wrote them down verbatim. Muslims believe that these original Gospels were lost and the current Gospels of the New Testament were altered by Jesus' followers and contain errors (Noegel & Wheeler, 2003; Bennett, 2008). Muslims believe the Qur'an, as noted above, is the last and final divine scripture, correcting all errors in earlier scriptures that were corrupted or lost ("This is the Scripture in which there is no doubt…" (2:2). Likewise, Islam is considered the final religion ("It is He who has sent His Messenger with guidance and the religion of truth, to show that it is above all [other] religions…") (9:23).

Belief in the Day of Judgement
Muslims believe that there will be a Day of Judgment when the world ends and all humans (dead and alive) will be judged for their deeds. Some will then spend eternity in the bliss of heaven: "[But] you, soul

at peace: return to your Lord well pleased and well pleasing; go in among My servants; and into My garden" (89:27-30). Others, however, will be consigned to another place for eternity: "God will not forgive those who have disbelieved and do evil, nor will he guide them to any path except that of hell, where they will remain forever…" (4:168-169). According to the Qur'an, only God knows when this Day of Judgment will occur (33:63), the day is not dependent on the Prophet Muhammad (6:57), everyone will recognize each other at that time (10:45), and all will be resurrected and judged (17:49). The Qur'an describes the Day as follows: "On that Day, people will come forward in separate groups to be shown their deeds: whoever has done and an atom's -weight of good will see it, but whoever has done an atom's-weight of evil will see that" (99:6-8). Just prior to the Day of Judgment, the Mahdi ("guided one") will appear and begin a 5-19 year period of justice, establishment of the true religion (Islam) throughout the world, and then the end will come. Muslims believe that Jesus (Isa or Iesa) will reappear that this time: "And he ['Iesa (Jesus), son of Maryam (Mary)] shall be a known sign for (the coming of) the Hour (Day of Resurrection) [i.e. 'Iesa's (Jesus) descent on the earth]. Therefore have no doubt concerning it (i.e. the Day of Resurrection)…"(43:61).[1,2] He will assist the Mahdi against the *Al-Masīh ad-Dajjāl* (deceiver or evil one) (Yahya, 2010). While the Qur'an states that judgement will be severe for the disbelievers on this Day, it also emphasizes God's mercy and forgiveness for those who turn to him: "We shall certainly blot out the misdeeds of those who believe and do good deeds, and we shall reward them according to the best of their actions" (29:7).

Belief in Angels
Angels are supernatural beings who serve God. They are not human or previously human. Angels are considered subordinate to humans,

---

[1] Translation by Muhammad Taqi-ud-Din Al-Hilali and Muhammad Muhsin Khan (*The Noble Qur'an*. Riyadh, Saudi Arabia: King Fahd Complex, 1998); also see translations by Abdullah Yusuf Ali (*The Holy Quran*. London, UK: The Islamic Computing Centre, Lahore 1934-1937) and by Sheik Muhammad Sarwar (*The Holy Qur'an*. NY, NY: Imam Al Khoei Islamic Center, 1981)
[2] *Sahih al-Bukhari*, Volume 3, Book 43, Number 656 (all translations of Sahih Bukhari by M. Muhsin Khan (2009). *Sahih Bukhari*. Retrieved from http://d1.islamhouse.com/data/en/ih_books/single/en_Sahih_Al-Bukhari.pdf (accessed on 3/14/17)

since the Angels were asked to bow down to and prostrate themselves before Adam (2:30-34), which Iblis (Satan) refused to do and was therefore banished from Paradise for disobedience (7:11-18). Another angel, Gabriel (a good one), is believed to have appeared to the Prophet Muhammad in order to reveal the Qur'an and later to transport the Prophet to Jerusalem during the Night Journey (17:1, 53:13-18). The angel Michael is also described in the Qur'an as a messenger of God (2:98) along with the angel of death or malak al-maut (different from Iblis) (32:11). Both the angel Gabriel and the angel Michael are described in the Qur'an as message bearers from God (2:97-98; 66:4).

Belief in Destiny (*qadr*).
Muslims believe that everything, every event and circumstance in life, plays a part in God's will and purpose for the world. The Qur'an says, "It was not without purpose that We created the heavens and the earth and everything in between..." (38:27). The Qur'an is clear in stating that God's will is supreme, even above that of the human will: "No misfortune can happen, either in the earth or in yourselves, that was not sent down in writing before we brought it into being..." (57:22) and "So where are you [people] going? This is a message for all people; for those who wish to take the straight path. But you will only wish to do so by the will of God, the Lord of all people" (81:26-29). Nevertheless, the Qur'an also states that people have the freedom to choose to be good or not: "BEHOLD, from on high have We bestowed upon thee this divine writ, setting forth the truth for [the benefit of all] mankind. And *whoever chooses* to be guided [thereby], does so for his own good, and *whoever chooses* to go astray, goes but astray to his own hurt; and thou hast not the power to determine their fate" (39:41).[1] The belief in destiny is sometimes used to explain why some Muslims attribute their mental illness to "God's will," which may prevent them from seeking help and effective treatment. The misunderstanding of what "destiny" means may lead to wrong attitudes in this regard. See Acevedo (2008) for a full discussion of this topic. Regardless, Muslims seldom ask "Why me?," a question that is common in the West when adversity strikes (Hamdy, 2009).

---

[1] Translation by Muhammad Asad (2003). *The Message of the Koran*. Watsonville, CA: The Book Foundation

Conclusions

These six beliefs concerning God, the Prophets, Divine books, the Day of Judgement, Angels, and Destiny form the bedrock of the Islamic faith tradition. In order to provide therapy that is respectful of a client's beliefs, values and preferences (as required by the Joint Commission that accredits both outpatient and inpatient mental health care in the U.S.)[1], the therapist or clergy person needs to understand what those beliefs are. This is particularly important for Muslim clients whose lives (and mental health) often revolve around their religious beliefs.

---

[1] Joint Commission for the Accreditation of Hospital Organizations (JCAHO) Requirements, RI.01.01.01, EP6 (hospital and ambulatory versions). *The Joint Commission, E-dition®*. Oak Brook, Illinois: Joint Commission Resources, January 1, 2016

CHAPTER 4

ISLAMIC PRACTICES

Of the "five pillars of Islam," the Shahadah (confession of faith) is the first. The remaining four pillars have to do with religious practices: (1) daily prayer, (2) giving alms, (3) fasting during Ramadan, and (4) pilgrimage to Mecca (Hajj).[1] These four practices are termed "obligatory," meaning that all Muslims are expected to do them.

Daily Prayer (*Salat*)
Muslims are expected to pray five times daily, beginning at the age of 7 years. The times are specified and in many communities are announced by a call to prayer (adhaan) made over a loudspeaker from the top of the mosque. The five times are at dawn before sunrise (*al-fajr*), midday after the sun reaches its zenith (*al-zuhr*), late part of the afternoon (*al-'asr*), just after sunset (*al-maghrib*), and before midnight (*al-'isha*).

Praying is an elaborate process. First, Muslims must clean themselves before prayer (called *wudhu*), which involves washing the right, and then the left hand three times; cleansing the mouth three times; cleansing the nose by breathing in water gently and expelling it

---
[1] Sahih Bukhari 1:50, 2:480, 6:300

three times; cleansing the face from the top of the forehead to the chin and up to both ears three times; cleansing the arms up to the elbow three times, beginning with the right; cleansing the head by passing wet hands once from the beginning of the hairline and over the head; cleansing the back and inside of the ears; and cleansing the foot up to the ankle beginning with the right.

Second, Muslims must lay out their prayer mat towards Mecca and begin praying by saying "Allahu Akbar" ("God is [the] greatest"), while raising hands to the ears or shoulders. All statements are in Arabic throughout the prayer. Third, they must place their right hand over the left on the chest or navel while in the standing position and read a short statement glorifying God and seeking His protection, followed by Surah Al Fatiha (first chapter of the Qur'an). Fourth, they bow at a 45 degree angle and say "Glory be to God, the Most Great"(Sub'hana rabiyal adheem) which is said three times. Fifth, Muslims prostrate themselves with only the palms, knees, toes, forehead and nose touching the ground, while repeating "Glory be to God, the Most High" three times (a callous on the forehead where it touches the ground is evidence of a devout prayer life, see 48:29).

Sixth, they move to a sitting position and recite 'God is [the] Greatest" for a moment or two and then repeat it as they bow again with forehead and palms touching the ground as before, saying "Glory be to God, the Most High," which completes the unit (each prayer session repeats the complete unit at least twice). Seventh, Muslims repeat "God is Great" and return to the sitting position, where they recite a set of short prayers praising God, sending peace on the Prophet, repeating the declaration of faith as they raise the forefinger of their right hand signifying their witness. The prayer ends after they turn to the right saying "Peace be upon you, and the mercy and blessings of Allah" and repeat it again after turning to the left.

These movements can be made quite rapidly if attention is focused without distraction, and may take anywhere from 4-8 minutes (not counting the time washing, called ablution). Men are required to say the prayers at the mosque on Fridays, although women are usually encouraged to say the prayers at home.

Giving Alms (*Zakat* or *Zakah*)
Muslims are required to give 2.5% annually of all assets owned continuously throughout the year, including cash savings, agricultural goods, gold, silver, stocks, and livestock. Excluded from the calculation are a person's home, clothing, and household furniture. This is obligatory in Islam (based on 2:227, 3:92, and many other verses in the Qur'an). The Zakat is compulsory in Saudi Arabia, Libya, Malaysia, Pakistan, and Sudan, but voluntary elsewhere. Some Muslims, in addition to the Zakat, give alms voluntarily called *Sadaqah* (charity). Charity is highly emphasized in the Qur'an and many blessings are promised to those who give it (2:110; 2:261; 2:2777; 70:22-24).

Fasting during Ramadan (*Fard*)
Muslims are required to fast "so that you may be mindful of God" (2:183). Fasting is obligatory during the month of Ramadan from dawn till sunset based on the Quran 2: 185. It is required for anyone who is mentally healthy, reached the age of puberty, and does not have a health reason for not fasting. Fasting means completely restraining from all foods, drink, intercourse, and smoking during these hours. Avoiding all forms of consumption helps to focus the mind on prayer and worship and impacts a person's mood and mental state as well. There are also several non-obligatory fasts that may also be performed by Muslims at other times of the year (Wajib, Sunnah, Nafl, Makrooh, and Haram). Moderation, though, is emphasized. Muslims are encouraged not to over-eat (..."eat and drink [as We have permitted] but do not be extravagant: God does not like extravagant people") (7:31; see also 20:81) or to fast excessively ("Verily, your own self has rights over you, so fast and break your fast, pray and sleep") (Sunan Abī Dāwūd #1369).

Pilgrimage to Mecca (*Hajj*)
Muslims are obligated to make a pilgrimage to Mecca at least once during their lifetime if physically able and can afford to go (2:196). The Hajj (the largest pilgrimage in the world) takes place during the 12th month of the Islamic lunar calendar. Nearly two million Muslims go on the Hajj each year. During this time, pilgrims focus on their relationship with God and put behind them all of the problems causing stress in their lives (work, family, friendships). No improper

speech, arguing or bad remarks about others are allowed during this time, whereas healthy interactions and a focus on God are encouraged (2:197). There is also plenty of physical exercise with walking and some running. Everyone -- the rich, the poor, men, women, those from different countries and races – are considered equal before God during the Hajj. This increases community solidarity and gives a sense of being part of something much larger.

Conclusions

This chapter describes the practices that all Muslims are required to engage in (i.e., are obligatory) and those that are optional. Knowing about these practices (particularly the required daily prayer and fasting practices) will help mental health professionals and clergy to provide a comfortable and supportive environment in which to address the mental health needs of Muslim clients, whether that be in the outpatient clinic or inpatient hospital setting.

CHAPTER 5

ISLAMIC VALUES

Islamic values naturally emerge from Islamic beliefs and practices, and from Arabic tradition.

Respect for Human Life
Muslims consider human life to be precious and sacred in all its forms from embryo to advanced old age, regardless of whether a person is healthy, sick, or disabled. From this belief come the teachings concerning abortion, physician-assisted suicide, euthanasia, and suicide.

<u>Abortion</u>. Abortion is never permitted except under rare circumstances in Islam. According to the Qur'an, "Do not kill your children for fear of poverty -- We shall provide for them and for you -- killing them is a great sin" (17:31; 6:151). It doesn't matter whether the pregnancy was planned or not, or whether the baby will interfere with the mother's lifestyle, education, or career. It is not allowed when pregnancy results from adultery that is not coerced. The only exception after four months of pregnancy is if the pregnancy or delivery will cause grave risk to the mother's life (BBC, 2009). Abortion is forbidden after four months of pregnancy even if there is a confirmed untreatable fetal anomaly. All schools of Islamic law agree on this position.

<u>Assisted Suicide or Euthanasia</u>. Nowhere in Islamic law is the "right to die" found. Physician-assisted suicide, euthanasia, or the shortening of life for any reason is forbidden. Withdrawal of life support from a person determined to be in persistent vegetative state is not clear (Sarhill et al., 2001; Hassaballah, 1996). Life support, however, may be discontinued if only the equipment is keeping the person alive (although this must be clear). While do-not-resuscitate orders are permitted, even this is not straight forward (Rehman, 1993). The Qur'an is very clear on that physician-assisted suicide is strictly forbidden: "Do not kill each other, for God is merciful to you" (4:29), and "If anyone kills a believer deliberately, the punishment for him is Hell, and there he will remain: God is angry with him, and rejects him, and has prepared a tremendous torment for him" (4:93). A recent thorough discussion of end-of-life decision making that addresses ethical issues in Muslims that come up at this time can be found elsewhere (Chamsi-Pasha et al., 2017).

<u>Suicide</u>. Suicide is *haram* (forbidden) in Islam. The Qur'an and Hadith are clear on this. The Qur'an says: "…do not contribute to your destruction with your own hands, but do good, for God loves those who do good" (2:195). Likewise, the most respected and reliable of all Sunni Hadiths, *Sahih Bukhari*, indicates:

> "The Prophet said, 'He who commits suicide by throttling shall keep on throttling himself in the Hell Fire (forever) and he who commits suicide by stabbing himself shall keep on stabbing himself in the Hell-Fire'" (Bukhari 2/23/446).[1]
>
> "The Prophet said, 'Whoever purposely throws himself from a mountain and kills himself, will be in the (Hell) Fire falling down into it and abiding therein perpetually forever; and whoever drinks poison and kills himself with it, he will be carrying his poison in his hand and drinking it in the (Hell) Fire wherein he will abide eternally forever; and whoever kills himself with an iron weapon, will be carrying that weapon in his hand and stabbing his abdomen with it in the (Hell) Fire wherein he will abide eternally forever'" (Bukhari 7/71/670).

---

[1] We list the reference by volume, book, and number (vol/book/no). From 2009 translation M. Muhsin Khan. Retrieved from http://d1.islamhouse.com/data/en/ih_books/single/en_Sahih_Al-Bukhari.pdf (accessed on 3-14-17)

Family and Community
Besides faith in God, Muslims prioritize family relationships, kin and community responsibilities above all others. The Qur'an reinforces this in many places:

> "...Worship none but God; be good to your parents and kinfolk, to orphans and the poor; speak good words to all people..."(2:83)

> "They ask you [Prophet] what they should give. "Say," whatever you give should be for parents, close relatives, orphans, the needy, and travelers. God is well aware of whatever good you do" (2:215)

> "Worship God; join nothing to him. Be good to your parents, to relatives to orphans, to needy, two neighbors near and far, to travelers in need, and to your slaves" (4:36)

Children are responsible for respecting and supporting their parents, especially when old, which is considered a religious practice and a good deed to be rewarded here and in the afterlife:

> "… be kind to your parents. If either or both of them reach old age with you, say no word that shows impatience with them, and do not be harsh with them, but speak to them respectfully and lower your wing in humility towards them in kindness and say 'Lord, have mercy on them, just as they cared for me when I was little'" (17:23-24)

> "We have commanded man to be good to his parents… 'Lord, help me to be truly grateful for Your favors to me and to my parents…" (46:15)

Marriage

Marriage is sacred in Islam, and Muslims believe that God will reward those who marry and are faithful to their partner. While the Qur'an doesn't forbid celibacy, it does not encourage it. Says Islamic theologian Fazlur Rahman (1998, p 103): "The Qur'an definitely encourages marriage and discourages celibacy, but the general prevalent notion among Western scholarly circles that it prohibits celibacy is false." Similar to the care of parents, the Qur'an views marriage and care for the family as a religious practice: "Husbands should take good care of their wives, with [the bounties] God has given to some more than others and with what they spend out of their own money. Righteous wives are devout and guard what God would have them guard in their husbands' absence" (4:34). Thus, husbands are to care for their wives and wives are to safeguard whatever their husbands produce, whether the husband is present or not. Adultery is explicitly forbidden, as the marital bed is not to be defiled: "And do not go anywhere near adultery: it is an outrage, and an evil path" (17:32). The Qur'an prescribes severe punishment for doing so: ""Strike the adulteress and the adulterer one hundred times. Do not let compassion for them keep you from carrying out God's law -- if you believe in God and the Last Day -- and ensure that a group of believers witnesses the punishment" (24:2). Muslim men are allowed to have up to four wives, although they must treat each wife the same, which is difficult to do. The Qur'an says: "You will never be able to treat your wives with equal fairness, however much you may desire to do so…" (4:129). In reality, few Muslim men have more than one wife (5% or less in the Arab world on average) (Chamie, 1986; Ozkan et a., 2006).

Work

Islam encourages people to work and do their part, contributing to the support of the family and the community (Ahmad & Owoyemi, 2012). The Qur'an says: "Has he not been told what was written in the Scriptures of Moses and of Abraham, who fulfilled his duty: that no soul shall bear the burden of another; that man will only have what he has worked towards; that his labor will be seen and that in the end he will be repaid in full for it… (53:36-41). As a result, pride is taken in the ability to support oneself and others, and those who work hard and treat others with respect are admired and looked up to. Mohamad Kamal Hassan (1988) describes five attributes that characterize Islamic work values (cited in Ahmad & Owoyemi, 2012, and paraphrased here):

> 1. Employees must fulfill their jobs as a societal obligation with the purpose of serving God.
> 2. Trustworthiness as an earthly representative of God with regard to all aspects of living.
> 3. Perform their duties as if they were a religious obligation (again); doing so will be rewarded in the hereafter.
> 4. Workers must be diligent and efficient and fair as they serve the interests of the community.
> 5. The relationship between employer and employee must be based on the principle of equality, independent of ethnic background, language or wealth.

The Environment

The Qur'an emphasizes that people should not destroy the beautiful creation that God has placed humans in, and encourages them to clean up any contamination in the environment that may spoil it. Emari and colleagues (2017) list over 60 separate verses in the Qur'an on environmental consciousness, and have developed a 19-item scale (the Islamic Environmental Consciousness Scale) to assess this.

Treatment of Others and Self-Esteem

Individuals are judged in Islam only on things they have control over. All persons are equal regardless of tribe, language or country, except to the extent they choose to deviate from prescribed Islamic beliefs and practices and persist in doing so. This influences their emotions and self-esteem and may affect motivation toward self-improvement and toward prosocial activity, factors that could counteract feelings of worthlessness or lack of meaning and purpose in life.

Islam encourages downward comparisons with regard to possessions (comparing to those who are less fortunate), but upward comparisons regarding family, community, and theological matters, all of which promotes satisfaction and virtuous living. At the top are values such as faith, fairness, justice, and care for the poor. These are all strongly supported by the Qur'an and encouraged for everyone, which helps to counteract inferiority and increase self-worth.

Self-esteem is very important to Muslims, particularly those from the Middle East and Arab world. Islam emphasizes that it is OK to make mistakes, but that we need to learn from them, not keep making the same mistakes over and over again. Muslims believe that God is tremendously merciful and ready to forgive, but there are consequences for repeatedly deviating from the life that is described in the Qur'an.

Positive Attitudes

The Qur'an promotes positive attitudes to everything that happens in life, even when things are not going well. Muslims are to always trust in God. The Qur'an says, "Who is it that answers the distressed when they call upon Him? Who removes their suffering? Who makes you successors in the earth? Is it another god beside God?" (27:62). Life on earth is described as a test (29:2-3), especially when hard times and trials come along. Islam encourages people to expect such trials, since all persons in every time period have had to deal with them (especially the Prophets): "Do you suppose that you will enter the Garden without first having suffered like those before you? If they were afflicted by misfortune and hardship, and they were so shaken that even their messenger and the believers with him cried "When will God help arrived?" Truly, God's help is near" (2:214).

Islam emphasizes that one of the greatest of sins is to give up because a person does not feel that God listens or cares. The Qur'an insists that God does care, and even if a person makes many mistakes, he or she can always be forgiven: "[Prophet] if My servants ask you about Me, I am near. I respond to those who call Me, so let them respond to Me, and believe in Me, so that they may be guided" (2:186). Such beliefs promote positive attitudes that increase motivation to push ahead in the face of hardship.

Conclusions

Muslims hold high values in terms of respect for human life, importance of the family, reverence for the sanctity of marriage, necessity of work and productivity, care for the environment, respect for others, and positive attitudes grounded on the belief that God has a purpose for everything. These values are likely to positively impact mental health in numerous ways that include reducing the frequency of stressful life events, coping with stressful life events when they occur, and having support from family and community to help when needed. These high values also place Muslims at higher risk of being disappointed in themselves when they fail to live up to these high expectations, possibly affecting risk for depression or anxiety. We examine this more closely in the next chapter.

CHAPTER 6

ISLAM AND MENTAL HEALTH:

SPECULATIONS

How might Islamic beliefs, practices, and values influence the mental health of Muslims? Here we speculate on possible positive and negative effects. These hypotheses will be tested by systematic research in the following chapter.

Positive Effects
Muslims believe that what is written in the Qur'an is God speaking directly to them. Table 1 and Table 2 present a sample of verses from the Qur'an and the Hadith (sayings of the Prophet Muhammad) that relate to mental, behavioral, and social health. The Qur'an encourages believers to live in harmony with others, thus enhancing social relationships and ensuring that others will be around to provide psychological support when needed: "Seek the life to come by means of what God granted you, but do not neglect your rightful share in this world. Do good to others as God has done good to you. Do not seek to spread corruption in the land, for God does not love those who do this" (28:77).

The Qur'an places emphasis on fairness, forgiveness, and mercy, which might be expected to address issues related to guilt and holding grudges. For example, while the Qur'an promises swift and severe punishment for disbelief and sin, forgiveness is readily available: "But if you avoid the great sins you have been forbidden, we shall wipe out your minor misdeeds and let you in through the entrance of honor" (4:31) and "Say, '[God says], My servants who have harmed yourselves by your own excess, do not despair of God's mercy. God forgives all sins: He is truly the Most Forgiving, the Most Merciful" (39:53). Finally, the high value that Muslims place on family and community, work, putting people before possessions, and positive attitudes, as noted in the last chapter, should enhance mental health and well-being. How do Muslim beliefs and values, then, apply to specific mental health issues such as depression, suicide, anxiety, substance use/abuse, and chronic mental illness?

Depression. There are many verses in the Qur'an that address issues related to mood. The Prophet Muhammad himself probably suffered from various mood states while being marginalized, excluded, and persecuted for his revolutionary religious teachings, a time when both his wife and his uncle who raised and supported him died. It was during this period that the following verse was revealed:

> "By the morning brightness and by the night when it grows still, your Lord has not forsaken you [Prophet], nor does He hate you, in the future will be better for you than the past; your Lord is sure to give you so much that you will be well satisfied. Did He not find you an orphan and shelter you? Did He not find you lost and guide you? Did He not find you in need and make you self-sufficient?... talk about the blessings of your Lord" (93:1-8, 11).

This emphasis on the blessings of the Lord is important to note, since a focus on positive aspects of life and avoidance of negative ruminations is central to how cognitive behavioral therapy (CBT) for depression works. Likewise, the Qur'an emphasizes that God's help is always available: "So truly where there is hardship there is also ease; truly where there is hardship there is also ease. The moment you are free [of one task], work on, and turn to your Lord for everything" (94:5-8).

Table 1. Verses on mental, behavioral, and relational health in the Qur'an

Coping with Illness (physical and mental)
"If God touches you [Prophet] with affliction, no one can remove it except Him, and if He touches you with good, He has power over all things: He is te Supreme Master over His creatures, the All Wise, the All Aware" (6:17-18)

Depression
"People, a teaching from your Lord has come to you, a healing for what is in [your] hearts, and guidance and mercy for the believers. Say [Prophet], 'In God's grace and mercy let them rejoice: these are better than all they accumulate.'" (10:57-58)

"We send down the Qur'an as healing and mercy to those who believe…" (17:82)

Self-condemnation
"No blame will be attached to the blind, the lame, the sick" (24:61)

Forgiveness
"Prophet, when believing women come and pledge to you that they will not ascribe any partner to God, nor steal, nor commit adultery, nor kill their children, nor lie about who has fathered their children, nor disobey you in any righteous thing, then you should accept their pledge of allegiance and pray to God to forgive them: God is most forgiving and merciful" (60:12)

Suicide
"…do not contribute to your destruction with your own hands, but do good, for God loves those who do good" (2:195)

Table 1. Verses on mental, behavioral, and relational health in the Qur'an (continued)

Eating Disorder
"'Eat from the good things We have provided for you, but do not overstep the bound, or my wrath will descend on you" (20:81)[1]

Substance Use and Gambling
"They ask you [Prophet] about intoxicants and gambling: say, 'There is great sin in both, and some benefit for people: the sin is greater than the benefit'" (2:219)

"You who believe, intoxicants and gambling, idolatrous practices, and [diving with] arrows are repugnant acts -- Satan's doing-- shun them so that you may prosper. With intxicants and gambling, Satan seeks only to incite enmity and hatred among you, and to stop you remembering God and prayer." (5:90-91)

Proper Use of Money
"Spend in God's cause: do not contribute to your destruction with your own hands, but do good for God loves those who do good" (2:195)

---

[1] Muhammad Asad translates 20:81 as: "Partake of the good things which We have provided for you as sustenance, but do not transgress therein the bounds of equity lest My condemnation fall upon you"

Table 2. Mental, behavioral, and relational health in the Sunni Hadith (from Sahih al-Bukhari, vol 7, book 71)

Hope
"The Prophet said, 'There is no disease that Allah has created, except that He also has created its treatment.'" (582)

Bereavement and Grief
"Aisha used to recommend At-Talbina for the sick and for such a person as grieved over a dead person. She used to say, 'I heard Allah's Apostle saying, 'At-Talbina gives rest to the heart of the patient and makes it active and relieves some of his sorrow and grief.''" (593)[1]

Suicide
"The Prophet said, 'Whoever purposely throws himself from a mountain and kills himself, will be in the (Hell) Fire falling down into it and abiding therein perpetually forever; and whoever drinks poison and kills himself with it, he will be carrying his poison in his hand and drinking it in the (Hell) Fire wherein he will abide eternally forever; and whoever kills himself with an iron weapon, will be carrying that weapon in his hand and stabbing his abdomen with it in the (Hell) Fire wherein he will abide eternally forever.'" (670)

Fear and Anxiety
"The prophet ordered me or somebody else to do Ruqya (if there was danger) from an evil eye." (634)[2]

"Allah's Apostle used to treat with a Ruqya saying, 'O the Lord of the people! Remove the trouble. The cure is in Your Hands, and there is none except You who can remove it (the disease).'" (640)

---

[1] *At-Talbina* is made from barley flour, milk and honey
[2] *Ruqya* involves reciting words from the Holy Qur'an to treat illness (including mental ilnness)

Table 2. Mental, behavioral, and relational health in the Sunni Hadith (from Sahih al-Bukhari, vol 7, book 71) (continued)

Fear and Anxiety
"Allah's Apostle said, 'Avoid the Mubiqat, i.e., shirk and witchcraft.' " (659)[1]

Maintaining Mental Health
"Whenever Allah's Apostle went to bed, he used to recite Surat-al-Ikhlas, Surat-al-Falaq and Surat-an-Nas and then blow on his palms and pass them over his face and those parts of his body that his hands could reach. And when he fell ill, he used to order me [Aisha, his wife] to do like that for him." (644)[2]

---

[1] *Mubiqat* means "destructive sins," including *shirk*, which involves worshiping anything other than God

[2] Here are the words in the Qur'an for these verses:
"Say, 'He is Allah , [who is] One, Allah , the Eternal Refuge. He neither begets nor is born, Nor is there to Him any equivalent' " (*Surat-al-Ikhlas* 112:1-4)
"Say, 'I seek refuge in the Lord of daybreak From the evil of that which He created And from the evil of darkness when it settles And from the evil of the blowers in knots And from the evil of an envier when he envies' " (*Surat-al-Falaq* 113:1-5)
"Say, 'I seek refuge in the Lord of mankind, The Sovereign of mankind. The God of mankind, From the evil of the retreating whisperer - Who whispers [evil] into the breasts of mankind - From among the jinn and mankind.' " (*Surat-an-Nas* 114:1-6)

Positive Effects (Depression, continued)

The Qur'an also stresses the need to be thankful: "Remember that He promised, 'If you are thankful, I will give you more, but if you are thankless, my punishment is terrible indeed'" (14:7; see also 2:172, 2:185). Muslims believe that God does not want believers to feel sad or carry a heavy burden: "…God wants ease for you, not hardship. He wants you to complete the prescribed period and to glorify him for having guided you, so that you may be thankful" (2:185). Being thankful is known to be a powerful antidote to depression (Lin, 2015).

The performance of righteous deeds is another way to counteract depression, as the Qur'an promises joy (13:29), a great reward (17:9), and hope (18:46) as a result. Believers are encouraged never to give up hope, since God is always there to help: "…do not despair of God's mercy -- only disbelievers despair of God's mercy" (12:87) and "…God will find a way out for those who are mindful of Him, and will provide for them from an unexpected source; God will be enough for those who put their trust in Him…" (65:2-3).

<u>Suicide</u>. Murder is forbidden in Islam. The Qur'an says, "Do not kill each other, for God is merciful to you. If any of you does these things, out of hostility and injustice, We shall make him suffer Fire: that is easy for God" (4:29).

Likewise, as noted earlier, the Qur'an says "…do not contribute to your destruction with your own hands, but do good, for God loves those who do good" (2:195). The desire for death by a Muslim is discouraged even when physically ill and suffering, no matter how severe that suffering. Muslims believe that only God has the right to take a human life (except during war, when defending one's own life or defending the life of another). Rahman (1998, p 60) explains this attitude: "Sick people, as indeed healthy ones too, are strongly prohibited from desiring or praying for death, let alone committing suicide; for if a person is good, he may do more good if he lives longer, and if a person is not good, longer life may afford him a chance for conversion."

<u>Anxiety</u>. The Qur'an promises peace to those who focus on and trust in God: "those who have faith and whose hearts find peace in the remembrance of God—truly it is in the remembrance of God that hearts find peace" (13:28). In Islam, doing good deeds is important for experiencing that peace: "They shall have the Home of

Peace with their Lord, and He will take care of them as a reward for their deeds" (6:127). The Qur'an also says, "But God invites everyone to the home of peace, and guides whoever He will to a straight path. Those who did well will have the best reward and more besides. Neither darkness nor shame will cover their faces: these are the companions in paradise and there they will remain" (10:25-26).

The Qur'an assures Muslims who experience fear or guilt that God is always near and ready to be merciful, if they are willing to change their ways: "Call on your Lord humbly and privately— he does not like those who transgress His bounds: do not corrupt the earth after it has been set right— call on Him fearing and hoping. The mercy of God is close to those who do good" (7:55-56). The Qur'an also encourages those who are anxious to call on God: "Call on me and I will answer you…" (40:60). Muslims are also instructed to read the Qur'an, which has the answers to whatever they are struggling with: "People, a teaching from your Lord has come to you, a healing for what is in [your] hearts, and guidance and mercy for the believers" (10:57).

Finally, the Qur'an insists that putting trust in God is the answer to any and all problems: "God will be enough for those who put their trust in Him…" (65:3). Indeed, according to Bowlby (1952), a secure attachment (in his case, attachment to God) should result in greater well-being, less anxiety, and overall better coping.

<u>Substance Use/Abuse</u>. The use of intoxicants (alcohol or drugs) is forbidden in Islam. The Qur'an explains: "You who believe, do not come anywhere near the prayer if you are intoxicated, not until you know what you are saying…" (4:43). Besides interfering with prayer and one's focus on God, intoxicants may also cause fighting among the faithful, preventing them from serving God during times of war and peace: "You who believe, intoxicants and gambling…are repugnant acts -- Satan's doing -- shun them so that you may prosper. With intoxicants and gambling, Satan seeks only to incite enmity and hatred among you, and to stop you remembering God in prayer…" (5:90-91).

Although not mentioned in the Quran, illicit drugs are intoxicants that fog the mind: "Narrated Aisha [wife of the Prophet], Ummul Mu'minin: I heard the Messenger of Allah say: Every intoxicant is forbidden; if a faraq of anything causes intoxication, a handful of it is forbidden" (Sunan Abu Dawud 26:3679)[1]. This also applies to cigarette smoking because it is harmful to the body (based on the Qur'an 7:157). Consequently, Islamic scholars have unanimously forbidden smoking (Permanent Committee of Academic Research and Fatwa, Saudi Arabia, Fatwa No: 15928, Part 13, p 62).

<u>Chronic Mental Illness</u>. Although the Qur'an does not say much about chronic mental illness (other than perhaps "God does not burden any soul with more than it can bear" in 2:286), there are sayings of the Prophet Muhammad documented in the Hadith that address this to some extent. According to a well-known Hadith, "The Prophet said, 'There is no disease that Allah has created, except that He also has created its treatment'" (Bukhari 7/71/582).

In Islam, those with chronic severe mental illness are excused from their actions. According to a Hadith (recorded in Abu Dawud #4403 and Ibn Majah #2041), the Prophet Muhammad said: "The pen is lifted (stopped from writing the deeds) from three: the sleeping person until he wakes up, the handicapped or insane person till he becomes able to reason, and the child till he grows up (reaches the age of puberty)."

Finally, according to another Hadith, "Anas ibn Malik narrates that: A woman, who had a defect in her brain, said: 'Allah's Messenger, I want to talk to you.' He said: 'Mother of so and so, choose on which side of the road you would like to stand and talk, so that I may fulfill your need.' He stood with her on the sidewalk until she spoke to her heart's content" (Sahih Muslim, source unknown). Thus, the Prophet Muhammad sets an example of being compassionate towards those with chronic mental illnesses such as schizophrenia and other illnesses of the brain.

Negative Effects

Misunderstanding of Islamic teachings in the Qur'an and Hadith also have the potential to generate or worsen emotional illnesses in those who are vulnerable. Indeed, the punishments promised to those who do not abide by Islamic teachings are severe, and thus may promote guilt, anxiety, or stigma. For example, Muslims may be anxious over not having done enough good deeds to outweigh their bad deeds, given the strong emphasis on good deeds in the Qur'an. The Quran promises that on the Judgement Day everyone's deeds, good and

---

[1] English translation, *Sunan Abu Dawud*, 27, Drinks (Kitab Al-Ashribah). Retrieved from https://sunnah.com/abudawud/27 (last accessed 1/1/17)

bad, will be laid out before them and weighed. Those whose good deeds outweigh their bad deeds will go one place, and those whose bad deeds outweigh their good deeds go to another place. Consider the following verses from the Qur'an:

> "On that Day, people will come forward in separate groups to be shown their deeds: whoever has done an atom's-weight of good will see it, but whoever has done an atom's-weight of evil will see that (99:6-8).

> "The one who's good deeds are heavy on the scales will have a pleasant life, but the one who's good deeds are light will have the Bottomless Pit for his home" (101:6-9).

> "On that Day when the Trumpet is blown [Judgement Day], the ties between them will be as nothing and they will not ask about each other: those whose good deeds weigh heavy will be successful, but those whose balance is light will have lost their souls forever and will stay in Hell— the Fire will scorch their faces and their lips will be twisted in pain" (23:101-104).

Hell as described in the Qur'an is a terrible place, one that could evoke much fear and anxiety. While the descriptions are to motivate people to change their ways and live a life submitted to God, they could contribute to pathological anxiety to those who have these tendencies to begin with.

> "We shall send those who reject our revelations to the fire. When their skins have been burned away, we shall replace them with new ones so that they may continue to feel the pain…"(4:56)

> "…The guilty person will wish he could save himself from the suffering of that Day by sacrificing his sons, his spouse, his brother, the kinsfolk who gave him shelter, and everyone on earth, if it could save him. But no! There is a raging flame that strips away the skin, and it will claim everyone who rejects the truth, turns away" (70:11-17).

"...Garments of fire will be tailored for those who disbelieve; scalding water will be poured over their heads, melting their insides as well as their skins; there will be iron crooks to restrain them; whenever, in their anguish, they tried to escape, they will be pushed back in and told, 'Taste the suffering of the Fire'" (22:19-22).

Also, it may be difficult for some Muslims to understand why a person has severe mental illness or is otherwise suffering emotional problems when the Qur'an explicitly states:

"those who have faith and whose hearts find peace in the remembrance of God— truly it is in the remembrance of God that hearts find peace— those who believe and do righteous deeds: joy awaits these and their final homecoming will be excellent" (13:28-29).

"He responds to those who believe and doing good deeds, and gives them more of his bounty... Whatever misfortune befalls you [people], it is because of what your hands have done—God forgives much--you cannot escape him anywhere on earth... (42:26, 30).

If peace, joy and bounty are the rewards for remembering God and having faith and doing good deeds, then the reverse should also be true. Indeed, the Qur'an says as much – "it is because of what your hands have done" (42:30). In other words, those who are sad or anxious may be viewed as not having enough faith, not doing good deeds, or not following the teachings of the Qur'an. Those with emotional problems such as depression or anxiety problems, then, may be criticized, blamed for their problems, and consequently excluded from society or discriminated against. This, of course, is true for all religions that hold to high moral values and promise benefits for those who follow the teachings of that religion.

Finally, some Muslims may pick out verses from the Qur'an and use them to push their extreme agendas (while ignoring other verses that moderate these teachings). This may be done to justify harming others who do not believe as they do or who oppose their ideas. Desire for power and control may cause such psychopathic individuals to distort Islamic teachings to further their own selfish gains. The result is worldwide terrorism and manipulation of vulnerable people whom these individuals prey on and indoctrinate to serve their ends.

Conclusions

Islamic beliefs, practices and values have the potential to have both positive effects on mental health and negative effects. When rightly understood, Islamic teachings may help to guide life and provide tremendous peace and meaning in the face of adversity. When misunderstood, though, the opposite is possible. It is essential for mental health professionals to keep in mind both of these possibilities, since positive and negative effects may be present in the same individual. However, these are just speculations. In the next chapter, we examine systematic unbiased quantitative research that has put these possibilities to the test.

CHAPTER 7

ISLAM AND MENTAL HEALTH:

THE RESEARCH

Do the benefits of Islam and positive effects on mental health outweigh the potential negative effects? What is the mental health of Muslims compared to members of other religious groups or those with no religious affiliation? Is level of religiosity among Muslims related to their mental health and is that relationship positive or negative? Systematic research can help to answer such questions.

Summarized here is a systematic review of research published prior to 2010 (Koenig et al., 2012), along with examples of studies published since 2010 that provide a sampling of more recent research (Center for Spirituality, Theology and Health, 2017). We will focus here on religious coping, depression, suicide, anxiety, substance use, chronic mental illness, and psychological well-being more generally.

Use of Religion to Cope
Qualitative studies in the literature indicate that Muslims often use their religious beliefs to cope with stresses of all kinds. In a 2012 systematic review of research conducted around the world on religious coping (Koenig et al., 2012), 2.4% of studies (11 of 454) were conducted in Muslims. Prevalence rates of religious coping

(when participants were asked directly) were 80% and 100% depending on the particular sample. Participants ranged from parents of children with cancer in the United Arab Emirates (Eapen and Revesz, 2003), to residents of Afghanistan coping with war (Scholte et al., 2004), to children in Indonesia dealing with a terrifying tsunami (Hestyanti, 2006). One study examined the coping behaviors of patients with paranoid schizophrenia in Jordan and Germany (Conrad et al., 2007), finding that 29% in Jordan spontaneously (without being asked) mentioned religion as a coping factor compared to 0% of German patients.

Since that review in 2010, research examining religious coping in Muslims has dramatically increased. For example, Nurasikin and colleagues (2013) surveyed psychiatric outpatients in Kuala Lumpur, Malaysia, finding that private religious activities used to cope with illness were related to significantly less depression, anxiety and stress. In a study of hemodialysis patients in Tehran, Iran (Saffari et al., 2013), higher levels of religious coping were associated with greater quality of life and better physical health status. Finally, in a survey of 266 women with breast cancer in Iran (Khodaveirdyzadeh et al., 2016), participants were asked to rate religious coping practices on a scale from 0-3. Here are their responses: seeking help through prayer (2.97 average out of maximum 3.00), remembering God (2.81), doing everything possible and then leaving it up to God (2.72-2.85), appealing to the Prophet and Imams (2.75), attending a pilgrimage (2.69), reading certain prayers (2.60), and reading the Qur'an (2.31). These religious coping practices were related to better adjustment to cancer.

Depression

Given that depression is one of the most common mental disorders in the world, one of the most disabling (Whiteford et al., 2013), and causes more decline in health than chronic diseases such as heart problems, arthritis, asthma, or diabetes (Moussavi et al., 2007), this condition deserves special attention. Because there is rationale for expecting that depression might be either less or more prevalent among Muslims, research in this area should be particularly relevant to mental health professionals. Again, the research presented here is based on a systematic review of the literature prior to the year 2010, and a selective review of more recent studies. First, Muslims and non-Muslims will be compared on rates of depression and depressive symptoms; second, the relationship between religiosity and depression in Muslim populations will be examined; and third, the results of randomized clinical trials of religious interventions tested in depressed Muslims will be reviewed.

<u>Muslims vs. Non-Muslims</u>. Of three studies that compared Muslims and non-Muslims on depression, two found less depression among Muslims compared to Christians in Belgium (Friedman & Saroglou, 2010) and non-Muslims in United Arab Emirates (Hamdan & Tamim, 2011), and one study found more depression in Muslims (college students in Kuwait vs. college students in New Jersey) (Abdel-Khalek & Lester, 2010).

<u>Religiosity within Muslims</u>. In the systematic review conducted prior to 2010 and selected studies representing more recent research, 17 studies were identified that quantitatively measured religious involvement and depressive symptoms (Koenig & Al Shohaib, 2014, p 135). Of those, 12 (71%) found less depression among Muslims who were more religious; one study (6%) reported more depression in the more religious (indirectly affecting mood through perceived intolerance and anger in a study of Muslim immigrants in Belgium); and the remaining four studies found no association. These findings are somewhat more favorable than the 61% of studies reporting inverse relationships and 6% reporting positive relationships in Christians.

<u>Randomized Clinical Trials (RCTs)</u>. All three RCTs prior to 2010 examining psychotherapy for depression that included a religious component found it was superior to non-religious interventions in Muslim patients (Azhar & Varma, 1995a,b; Razali et al., 1998). A more recent RCT also found that reciting the Qur'an significantly reduced depressive symptoms among Muslim hemodialysis patients compared to controls (Babamohamadi et al., 2016).

Suicide
Suicide is the most feared consequence of depression, and most suicides occur in those who are depressed, particularly when depression is comorbid with substance abuse disorders (Tondo et al., 1999). Anywhere between 2% and 15% of depressed persons end their lives by suicide (Guze & Robins, 1970; Bostwick & Pankratz, 2000). In our systematic review conducted prior to 2010 and

selective review conducted since 2010 (Koenig & Al Shohaib, 2014, pp 140-141), seven studies compared suicide rates in Muslims vs. non-Muslims and nine studies examined the relationship between religiosity and suicide attitudes, attempts, and completed suicide in Muslims.

<u>Muslims vs. Non-Muslims</u>. Muslim-majority countries have some of the lowest reported suicide rates in the world. However, given the strong religious and cultural prohibitions against suicide, this may be partly attributed to under-reporting (Pritchard & Amanullah, 2007). Of the seven studies that compared Muslims and non-Muslims, three reported more negative attitudes, fewer attempts or lower suicide (Levav & Aiesenberg, 1989; Shah & Chandia, 2010; Gal et al., 2012), and one study found the opposite (college students in Turkey had more suicidal ideation than college students in America) (Gencoz et al., 2007).

<u>Religiosity within Muslims</u>. Of nine studies examining relationships between religiosity and suicidal ideation, attempts, or completion in Muslims, seven (78%) found an inverse relationship, and two studies reported no association. These findings are similar to those found in Christian populations, where 79% during this same period of review reported inverse relationships between religiosity and suicide.

Anxiety

Many studies have compared Muslims and non-Muslims on level of anxiety (seven studies), or have examined the relationship between religiosity and anxiety in Muslim populations (24 studies) (Koenig & Al Shohaib, 2014, pp 148-150).

<u>Muslims vs. Non-Muslims</u>. Of seven studies comparing anxiety in Muslims and non-Muslims, six (86%) reported more anxiety in Muslims (Yorulmaz et al., 2009; Abdel-Khalek, 2003; Tomas-Sabado & Gomez-Benito, 2004; Abdel-Khalek & Tomas-Sabado, 2005; Ellis et al., 2013; Inozu et al. 2012), supporting the claim that Islamic beliefs might make some adherents more anxious.

<u>Religiosity within Muslims</u>. While most studies suggest that Muslims are more anxious than non-Muslims, this appears to be true only in Muslims who are less religious. Of 24 cross-sectional studies, 15 (63%) reported inverse relationships between religiosity and anxiety in Muslim populations. In other words, the majority of

studies show that Muslims who are more religious are less anxious. This percentage of studies showing less anxiety in religious Muslims is in fact higher than that reported in religious Christians (49%).

<u>Randomized Clinical Trials</u>. There have also been at least four RCTs examining the effects of religiously-integrated psychotherapies for anxiety in Muslims, with all four (100%) reporting a reduction in anxiety significantly greater than for secular psychotherapies or standard care (Azhar et al., 1994; Razali et al., 1998; Razali et al., 2002; Hosseini et al., 2013). A fifth more recent clinical trial has also found that reciting the Qur'an dramatically reduces anxiety symptoms in Iranian hemodialysis patients compared to hemodialysis patient control (BabaMuhammadi et al., 2015). This suggests that psychotherapies designed to increase religiosity or utilize religiosity as a resource appear to be effective in reducing anxiety in Muslims, more so than therapies that ignore religious beliefs.

Substance Use/Abuse

Twelve studies compared alcohol use/abuse in Muslims with that in Christians and other religious groups, and six studies did so for drug use/abuse. In addition, our systematic review (prior to 2010) uncovered two studies that examined the relationship between religiosity and alcohol use in Muslim majority countries, two were identified that were missed by the review, and two more recent studies make a total of six (Koenig & Al Shohaib, 2014, p 154). These same six studies also examined drug use/abuse.

<u>Muslims vs. Non-Muslims</u>. With regard to alcohol use, nine of 12 studies (75%) reported significantly less alcohol use in Muslims compared to non-Muslims, and three of six studies found less drug use/abuse in Muslims compared to Christians and other religious groups (the remaining three studies, all comparing Muslims and Christians in Nigeria, found no difference).

<u>Religiosity within Muslims</u>. Of the six studies that examined religiosity and alcohol use/abuse or drug use/abuse, all six (100%) found significantly lower use among Muslims who were more religious. Although these findings are expected, given the strong prohibitions against intoxicants in the Qur'an, objective research confirms this.

Chronic Mental Illness

Chronic psychotic disorders such as schizophrenia, bipolar disorder, and delusional disorder are among the most common and disruptive of mental illnesses that adversely affect quality of life. Unfortunately, there has not been much research examining these disorders in Muslims compared to non-Muslims. Only three such studies were identified in the systematic and selective reviews. The same is true for research examining the relationship between psychosis and religiosity in Muslims, where we could identify only four studies (Koenig & Al Shohaib, p 154).

<u>Muslims vs. Non-Muslims</u>. Azhar and colleagues (1995) found a high prevalence of religious and culture-related delusions in patients with schizophrenia in Malaysia (>60% Muslim), but did not compare rates in Muslims vs. non-Muslims. One study compared ways of coping with hallucinations among patients with schizophrenia in Saudi Arabia and the United Kingdom (UK), finding that those in Saudi Arabia were significantly more likely to cope using religious activities (43%) compared to those in the UK (3%) (Wahass & Kent, 1997). In a retrospective study of psychotic inpatients at a psychiatric hospital in Cairo, Egypt, from 1975 to 1996, Muslims were slightly less likely than Christians to have religious symptoms (delusions, hallucinations, preoccupations). Not surprisingly, Muslims were more likely to present with psychotic symptoms involving the Prophet Muhammad, whereas Christians were more likely to have delusions regarding Jesus and Christian saints (Atallah et al., 2001).

In a more recent study of nearly 3000 college students in Kenya, psychotic symptoms were compared between Protestants, Catholics, and Muslims. Muslims were 38% less likely than Protestants to have any psychotic experiences and 22% less likely to have visual hallucinations, although differences were not statistically significant (Ndetei et al., 2012). In summary, there is no evidence that Muslims are more likely to have psychotic symptoms than non-Muslims, but there is evidence that they are more likely to cope with those symptoms using religious practices.

<u>Religiosity within Muslims</u>. Of the four studies examining religiosity and psychosis in Muslims, two found an inverse relationship with psychosis and two found a positive relationship. Both studies finding more psychosis in highly religious Muslims were in psychiatric patients. One study compared hospitalized patients in

Cairo who had received "spiritual healing" (which they defined as excessive use of prayers, reading verses from the Qur'an, exorcism, etc.) with those who had not, finding that psychotic relapse was more common in those with spiritual healing experiences (Salib and Youakim, 2001). The other study in Muslim psychiatric inpatients in Pakistan reported more delusions of grandeur of a religious nature in religious patients compared to non-religious patients (Suhail & Ghauri, 2010). Of the other two studies, one involved a community sample of adults from 18 countries; they found that schizotypal traits were less frequent in Muslims who were more religious (Johnstone & Tiliopoulos, 2008). The other study found that Muslim psychiatric outpatients who had more daily spiritual experiences were more likely to adhere to their medication (Amr et al., 2013).

Psychological Well-being
Many studies have examined the relationship between religiosity and well-being in Muslims, although few have compared Muslims and non-Muslims in this regard. The systematic review of research prior to 2010 and the selective review since then identified 20 studies examining religiosity and well-being, but only one study compared Muslims and non-Muslims (Koenig & Al Shohaib, 2014, p 172).

<u>Muslims vs. Non-Muslims</u>. In the only study identified that compared the well-being of Muslims and non-Muslims, Kazarian (2005) surveyed Christian and Muslim students at the American University of Beirut, finding no difference in psychological well-being between the two groups.

To assess this question further, two international datasets were analyzed in order to compare Muslims and non-Muslims on happiness (Koenig, 2016, unpublished data). The first dataset, the International Social Survey Program (ISSP 2008), surveyed a random sample of 59,063 citizens ages 15 to 90 from 40 countries: Australia, Austria, Belgium - Flanders, Chile, Croatia, Cyprus, Czech Republic, Denmark, Dominican Republic, Finland, France, Germany, Great Britain, Hungary, Ireland, Israel, Italy, Japan, Latvia, Mexico, Netherlands, New Zealand, Northern Ireland, Norway, Philippines, Poland, Portugal, Russia, Slovakia, Slovenia, Spain, South Korea, South Africa, Sweden, Switzerland, Taiwan, Turkey, Ukraine, Uruguay, the United States of America, Venezuela, Taiwan, Japan, and South Korea. Interviews were conducted face-to-face, by telephone and by self-completed postal questionnaires. This dataset included 2,152 Muslims (**66% from Turkey**), 43,663 non-Muslims affiliated with other religions, and 12,237 persons not affiliated with any religious group.

The second dataset was the World Values Survey (WVS, 2005-2006), a random sample of 83,879 adults ages 18 to 85 from more than 80 countries (approximately 1000 per country using full probability sampling). Muslims primarily come from **Indonesia** (12.4%), **Iraq** (11.2%), **Egypt** 19.1%, and **Mali** (9.5%). The mode of data collection for WVS survey was in person face-to-face interviewing. This project was carried out by an international network of social scientists, with local funding for each survey. The sample included 14,447 Muslims, 52,791 non-Muslims, and 14,631 adults with no religious affiliation.

In the ISSP (2008), Muslims were significantly less likely than non-Muslims or those with no religious affiliation to say they were "very happy" (16.8% vs. 26.9% and 22.2%, respectively, p<0.0001) (**Table 3**). This was even true for those who indicated they were at least "somewhat religious;" again, Muslims were also less likely to say that they were "very happy" (17.7% vs. 28.8% and 28.4%, respectively, p<0.0001). On the other hand, Muslims were much more likely than non-Muslims or those with no religious affiliation to strongly agree that "religion helps people find inner peace or happiness" and to strongly agree that "religion helps people find comfort during sorrow or trauma." Similar findings were found in the WVS (2005-2006).

More recently, the 2017 World Happiness Report asked 3000 people in each of 155 countries to evaluate their current lives on a scale from 0 to 10, where 0 (worst possible life) to 10 (best possible life), and then ranked countries on happiness based on those scores (1 being the happiest country, 155 being the least happy country). Of the 16 countries whose populations were over 90% Muslim, 9 (56%) were ranked between 100 and 155, and only two received a rank between 1 and 50 (**Table 4**).

There are many reasons for lower happiness and well-being among Muslims, and the Islamic religion is not likely one of them. Many factors affect the mental health of Muslims including the cultural environment, historical events, slower scientific progress than in Western countries (despite initially being far ahead of the Western in terms of medicine and science), overly strict understanding of religious teachings, to name just a few. In fact, a recent United Nations report (AHDR, 2016) found increasing inequality (based on the Human Development Index) in Arab countries (Middle East and North Africa). Armed conflict was common in these regions (17% of the world's wars and 45% of the world's terrorist attacks, despite making up only 5% of the world's population) and the unemployment rate was twice that of the global average (30% vs. 14%) (United Nations Development Programme, 2016). Therefore, socioeconomic and environmental problems appear to be much more prevalent among the world's Muslim population, compared to other religious groups and those with no religious affiliation.

These socioeconomic and environmental problems likely explain the differences in well-being found here, not the Islamic religion. One things is for certain, though. Muslims who are more religious are happier and experience greater well-being and less anxiety.

<u>Religiosity and Well-being in Muslims</u>. Of the 20 studies identified in the literature, all 20 (100%) found significant positive relationships between religiosity and well-being in Muslims. These studies were conducted in Pakistan, Kuwait, Malaysia, Algeria, Saudi Arabia, Egypt, Lebanon and Qatar. Greater well-being in highly religious Muslims was present regardless of country or age of participants. Relationships between religiosity and well-being among Muslims in the ISSP and WVS datasets, however, were not as consistent. In the ISSP, happiness was not related to self-rated religiosity ($r=0.035$) or frequency of religious attendance ($r=-0.038$). In the WVS, importance of religion was unrelated to happiness ($r=0.002$) or satisfaction with life ($r=-0.01$); however, frequency of religious service attendance was positively and significantly related to greater happiness ($r=0.093$, $p<0.0001$, $n=13,343$) in Muslims.

Given that Muslims often turn to religion in order to cope with difficulties in life (i.e., religion becomes more important to them when they are distressed), this dynamic may conceal a positive relationship between religiosity and well-being for measures of religious importance in cross-sectional studies like the ISSP and WVS.

Table 3. Psychological well-being in Muslims compared with non-Muslims and those with no religious affiliation

	Muslims % (N)/Mean (SD)	Non-Muslims % (N)/Mean (SD)	No Affiliation % (N)/Mean (SD)
<u>International Social Survey Program 2008</u>	100.0 (2,152)	100.0 (43,663)	100.0 (12,237)
How happy are you? ("very happy")	16.8 (361) *[1]	26.9 (11,757)	22.2 (2,714) *[2]
Among those are at least "somewhat religious"			
Very happy	17.7 (319) *	28.8 (7,923)	28.4 (375) *
Religion helps people find inner peace/happiness			
Strongly agree	72.4 (1,522) *	33.5 (13,965)	12.1 (1,365) *
Among those at least "somewhat religious"			
Strongly agree	78.8 (1,399) *	42.2 (11,189)	24.9 (318) *
R helps people find comfort during sorrow/trauma			
Strongly agree	66.9 (1,396) *	37.7 (13,794)	17.9 (2,039) *
Among those at least "somewhat religious"			
Strongly agree	72.7 (1,281) *	45.6 (12,094)	33.6 (432) *
<u>World Values Survey 2005-2006</u>	100.0 (14,447)	100.0 (52,791)	100.0 (14,631)
Taking all things together, how happy?			
"Very Happy"	24.6 (3,653) *	29.3 (15,480)	26.9 (3,888) *
Among those where religion very/rather important			
Taking all things together, how happy?			
"Very Happy"	24.4 (3,494) *	29.8 (11,415)	30.5 (860) *
Satisfied with life as a whole			
(1=not satisfied, 10=very satisfied)	6.09 (2.57) * (n=14,707)	6.81 (2.30) (n=52,831)	6.94 (2.10) * (n=14,507)
Among those where religion very/rather important			
Satisfied with life as a whole			
(1=not satisfied, 10=very satisfied)	6.08 (2.58) * (n=14,200)	6.69 (2.35) (n=38,352)	6.89 (2.21) * (n=2,814)

*$p<0.0001$, Mantel-Haenszel χ^2 used to compare Muslims and other religious groups when outcome is ordinal, chi-square (χ^2) for categorical outcomes; Student's t-test for continuous outcomes between two groups; analysis of variance for continuous outcomes between 3 groups

[1] Difference between Muslims and non-Muslims; [2] difference between all 3 groups

Table 4. Countries with 90% or greater Muslim[1] ranked by overall happiness based on World Happiness Report 2017[2]

Country	% Muslim	Happiness Rank[3]
Happiest countries		
Norway	3.0	1
Denmark	4.1	2
Iceland	0.1	3
Switzerland	0.5	4
Finland	0.2	5
Netherlands	2.3	6
Canada	1.1	7
New Zealand	0.2	8
Australia	0.9	9
Sweden	1.7	10
Muslim countries		
Somalia	99.9	93
Morocco	99.9	84
Saudi Arabia	99.9	37
Afghanistan	99.8	141
Iran	99.6	108
Yemen	99.0	146
Iraq	98.9	117
Turkey	98.6	69
Niger	98.3	135
Algeria	98.2	53
Sudan	97.0	130
Uzbekistan	96.5	47
Pakistan	96.4	80
Syria	92.8	152
Bangladesh	90.0	110
Egypt	90.0	104

[1] Pew Research Center (2011). The future of the global Muslim population. Retrieved from http://www.pewforum.org/2011/01/27/the-future-of-the-global-muslim-population/ (accessed on 3/20/17)
[2] Helliwell J, Layard R, Sachs J (2017). World Happiness Report 2017. Retrieved from http://worldhappiness.report/ed/2017/ (accessed on 3/20/17)
[3] Where 1=most happy country, 155=least happy country)

Conclusions

Based on the research reviewed above, Muslims tend to experience less depression, are less likely to have positive attitudes toward or commit suicide, and are less likely to use or abuse alcohol or drugs. They have similar rates of psychosis compared to non-Muslims, although are more likely to experience anxiety (especially if not religious). The comfort derived from reading and reciting the Qur'an, frequent prayer, devout religious beliefs, and a strong and close knit family and community helps to explain improved coping and lower rates of depression and suicide. Islamic teachings "place the bar high" in terms of ethical values and expectations for behavior, while emphasizing dire consequences in the hereafter if these teachings are not followed. These teachings can easily be misunderstood.

This may help to explain the higher rate of anxiety among Muslims compared to non-Muslims. However, there are many other factors (socioeconomic, environmental, cultural, historical, armed conflict, discrimination) may be a better explanation for these cross-sectional associations, since randomized clinical trials that utilize Islamic religious interventions significantly reduce anxiety, not increase it. Furthermore, there is a greater likelihood that religiosity in Muslims is associated with less anxiety than in Christians (63% vs. 49% of studies). This suggests that higher anxiety found in Muslims is probably concentrated among Muslims who are less religious.

Based on analyses of large datasets here, psychological well-being (happiness and satisfaction in life) also appears to be somewhat lower in Muslims than in non-Muslims (and even lower than in those with no religious affiliation). However, like with anxiety, this is almost certainly due to greater socioeconomic and environmental stressors that Muslims around the world must deal with. Indeed, one might wonder what the well-being of Muslims would be if they did not have their religious faith to help them deal with these stressors. This is supported by the finding that greater religious involvement within Muslim populations is related to less depression, less suicide, less substance use/abuse, and greater well-being in many studies. Finally, nine out of nine randomized clinical trials (100%) report that Islamic interventions in Muslims improve levels of depression and anxiety more so than do secular treatments or control conditions, underscoring the benefits that this religious faith plays in healing.

CHAPTER 8

CLINICAL APPLICATIONS

What, then, does the mental health professional, pastoral counselor or clergy do with this information? The suggestions we make in this chapter are based on the evidence from research, clinical experience, and common sense. We begin this chapter with a series of three case vignettes[1] to illustrate the kinds of clinical encounters that mental health professionals and clergy are likely to have when seeking to help Muslim clients.

Case Vignette #1

> Miss A is a 36 year old single woman from Saudi Arabia with severe anxiety who presents for outpatient treatment. A brief spiritual history reveals that she is Muslim and from a very religious family. Although she has always been somewhat anxious, it appears that her anxiety worsened significantly after she had a conversation with one of her girlfriends about religious matters. Miss A was somewhat reluctant to talk about this with

---

[1] Details of these cases have been altered to protect the identity of the individuals being discussed

the therapist, a non-Muslim, but with gentle encouragement by the therapist, she began to describe that conversation. Her girlfriend had asked Miss A the following question. If Miss A was to die suddenly (from a car accident or medical problem), did she think she had done enough good deeds to outweigh her bad deeds on the Day of Judgement. This got her thinking, and in particular, got her to worrying. She had slacked off on her daily prayer, was not giving alms, had been to several parties that year where she consumed alcohol, and had given in to her boyfriend and had sex with him last month. Soon after the conversation, Miss A became convinced that her bad deeds probably outweighed her good deeds, and that Judgement Day would be a bad time for her. This worry began to consume her, interfering with sleep and even work. The therapist suggested a course of weekly cognitive-behavioral therapy to address her anxiety, and suggested breathing and relaxation exercises that she could practice at home.

Progress was slow. During one of the CBT sessions, the therapist (who had existence experience treating Muslims patients and was knowledgeable about Islam) asked Miss A's permission to utilize her religious beliefs to help with the therapy. Desperate for relief, Miss A readily agreed. The therapist asked her to come up with a list of "good deeds" that she might engage in between sessions, and suggested she bring in an English version of the Qur'an for their next session. On the following week, Miss A came to therapy with a list of deeds as requested and a copy of the Qur'an. The therapist asked her to turn to 2:277 and read it out loud: "Those who believe, do good deeds, keep up the prayer, and pay the prescribed alms will have their reward with their Lord; no fear for them…" The therapist then asked her to turn to 6:160 and read that verse: "Whoever has done a good deed will have it 10 times to his credit, but whoever has done a bad deed will be repaid only with its equivalent…" The therapist asked her to explain what these passages meant to her. After a brief discussion, Miss A let out a sigh, and said that she would try to do some good deeds before the next session. When the therapist saw her the following week, Miss A reported having started praying again and giving alms, and indicated that her anxiety symptoms were much better.

Case Vignette #2

Mrs. T is a 50 year old successful and determined business woman with a strong personality and clear vision. Several years ago her nephrologist diagnosed her with polycystic kidney disease, an inherited disease associated with kidney failure and eventually requiring hemodialysis. She knew everything about her kidney problems and that it would only be a matter of time before she would have to go onto dialysis or die from her disease. However, she did not allow her condition to stop her career, professional development or social relationships. Eventually, the day came when her kidneys failed, dialysis was required, and finally a kidney transplant became necessary. Even after this, however, she continued to pursue her career and came back stronger than ever. Mrs. T is a deeply religious woman, although when you first meet her, you would think that she is anything but religious. During her battle with kidney disease, however, she said her relationship with Allah became very close. A few years after she received her kidney transplant, the new kidney gradually began to fail – and this time it was more difficult than it had been the first time. She became depressed and started having physical symptoms of kidney failure, including poor concentration that forced her to stop working.

The combination of depression and kidney failure caused her nephrologist to admit her to the hospital where she stayed for three months. Her body weakened and she became more and more fragile to the point where she could barely talk due to her depression. The nephrologist was not optimistic about her recovery. He thought for sure that the illness would end her career and business. Therefore, he referred her to a therapist to help her with the depression. After several weeks of supportive therapy with little progress, and knowing from their initial session (when a spiritual history was taken) that Mrs. T was religious, the therapist asked her if she would be willing to allow the therapist to utilize her religious beliefs in the therapy. She agreed. The therapist inquired further about what beliefs and practices were particularly important to her. She indicated that prayer and reading from the Qur'an had been especially comforting to her in the past, but had stopped doing these regularly during the past several months. So, the therapist encouraged her to restart these religious practices focusing them on the specific problems she was dealing with. The therapist suggested that she recite in Arabic a chapter from the Qur'an, the Surta-al-Ikhlas ("Say, 'He is Allah, [who is] One, Allah, the Eternal Refuge. He neither begets nor is born, Nor is there to Him any equivalent'" (112:1-4). This, the therapist told her, was what the Prophet Muhammad would recite when he became ill (*Sahih al-Bukhari*, volume 7, book 71: 644). As she began to pray and recite from the Qur'an regularly, she found that her religious faith began to deepen and her feelings of being overwhelmed began to lessen. Her therapist encouraged these religious practices and since the therapist was also Muslim, even engaged in prayer with her on occasion during therapy sessions (when Mrs. T requested her to do this).

After several months of therapy, Mrs. T travelled to another Arabic country where she had close relatives who invited her to stay with them so that they could care for her. However, she frequently traveled back and forth to her home in Riyadh and remained in contact with the therapist. When her nephrologist saw her in his when she returned for a visit, he discovered to his surprise that her depression had dramatically improved. She appeared charming, happy, and was even back to work part-time. Though her body remained weak, her spirit was strong. In talking with her about how she was able to cope with all this, she told the nephrologist that it was her trust in Allah (supported and encouraged by her therapist) that was getting her through these extraordinarily difficult times and helped her to never give up or lose hope.

Case Vignette #3

Mr. M is in his late 30's and vice president of a large company, a position to which he had quickly advanced. He had a strong personality, was persistent, and was dedicated to his work. He also had a large family and many friends with good relationships. His goal was to become a community leader at a young age, and everything was on track for that to happen, as he had real charisma. Then one day he was out in the field checking on a company project. While traveling to a job site, his driver got into a catastrophic car accident. Mr. M was immediately taken to the nearest hospital in a coma. The doctors told his family that he would likely die from his injuries. Although he survived, he was left with a broken neck and quadriplegia, and could not move his arms or legs or eat without assistance. The doctors told him that he would likely be bed-ridden for the rest of his life.

Few situations are more difficult to cope with in life than the one that Mr. M found himself in. Initially, he was overwhelmed and fell into a deep depression. His physician referred him to a counselor to help him to adjust to his severe disability. The therapist took a careful spiritual history during his initial evaluation. Realizing that he had strong religious beliefs, he asked Mr. M if he would like to try religious form of therapy, which he readily agreed to. The therapist then implemented a religiously-integrated version of Islamic cognitive behavioral therapy (CBT), a form of psychotherapy firmly grounded on the Qur'an.

After 10 weekly sessions that involved daily homework practices including meditating on passages in the Qur'an, Mr. M gradually learned to cope with his disability and his depression began to improve. As his motivation returned, he learned to do many things using his wheel-chair. Soon, Mr. M had resumed his regular trips to Mecca (Hajj and Umrah), which he made three times per year. As his mood improved, he began to attend social functions again, such as weddings, funerals, and community get-togethers. Despite his disability, his religious faith (strengthened by the therapy) made him a bright light at these social events since he had not lost his charisma and was still very charming with a deep sincere smile. In addition, because of his position as a businessman in the community, Mr. M began to help resolve disputes between different people in the community. He would even contribute financially from his own funds to reach a peace accord between feuding parties. In spite of being in a wheel-chair, he would regularly go to the mosque to pray and worship.

When talking with Mr. M, his therapist – whom he would

continue to see periodically – noticed that he would frequently talk about his close relationship with Allah and how much he loved him. It was from this relationship, Mr. M maintained, that he derived his value as a person. In spite of his severe disability, Mr. M said that he felt good about himself because his self-esteem was grounded on this relationship. He believed that Allah had a purpose for his life, and that purpose is what kept his morale high and prevented him from feeling low or inferior to others. Although realistic about his disability, Mr. M shared with his therapist one day that since his accident he had discovered that life had more purpose than ever before. He believed that it was his duty to do as much good as he could, since he had many things that others did not have, including knowledge, money, and respect. He said, "I can cope with anything and any problem in my life if I am persistent and stay close to Allah and in Allah's will."

Response to Vignettes

These cases raise many questions. Should therapists depart from the standard secular approach to treatment by bringing religion into the therapy? In Case #1, despite little progress towards improvement, should the therapist have continued to encourage deep breathing and progressive relaxation, instruct her to be mindful and present centered, prescribe pleasant behaviors to distract her from her religious ruminations, and challenge her dysfunctional cognitions causing her anxiety (her religious belief)? Those methods were not working in this case. This raises a dilemma that is not easily resolved, and may depend on the particular client and the specific issue that the client is struggling with. Rather than improve Miss A's anxiety, bringing religion into the therapy may have increased it -- particularly in the long-term as her so called "dysfunctional" religious beliefs became more central to her life and continued to influence her emotional state in various ways. But are these religious beliefs really dysfunctional for this client from a deeply religious family whose support network is primarily her religious community? Might her resumption of doing "good deeds" over the long term actually led to a fuller, higher quality of life for Miss A?

What about Cases #2 and #3? In each instance, the therapist took a spiritual history and with permission, began to utilize the client's religious beliefs in therapy to help them to cope with the severe stressors that were driving their emotional distress. In Case #2, the therapist even participated with the client in a religious practice, seemingly going beyond the boundary of the therapist-client relationship. In most cases, the therapist should be supportive and encouraging, but remain neutral. However, since the patient had requested to pray with the therapist, they were of the same religion, and the client was coping with a specific situational stressor, there may be instances when such boundaries may be relaxed.

In Case #3, the therapist decided that religious CBT might be particularly effective in helping this client deal with his devastating disability. Unfortunately, there are no long-term follow-up studies of religiously-integrated psychotherapies in Muslims (beyond about three months) that incorporate religious beliefs into the treatment of emotional disorder. Nevertheless, based on the existing research reviewed above, randomized clinical trials in Muslims have at least in the short-term documented substantial benefits from such an approach.

The following recommendations are based on the evidence from systematic research identified earlier, our combined 50+ years of clinical experience treating Muslim patents, and just plain good common sense.

1. Take a Spiritual History

Whether or not a therapist utilizes a Muslim client's religious beliefs in therapy, a spiritual history should always be taken early in the treatment (on initial evaluation, or soon afterward). The purpose of the spiritual history is to identify the specific religious beliefs of the client, the importance of those beliefs to the client, the extent to which beliefs and practices are adhered to, the religious beliefs and religiosity of the client's family of origin, and the religious beliefs and religiosity of the client's support system. Beliefs about the Qur'an and to what extent it is authoritative in the client's life should also be explored. Finally, both good and bad experiences with religion across the client's life course should be asked about. This information will be invaluable in deciding on the treatment approach and in providing treatment that meets the minimum standard of showing respect for clients' personal beliefs and values (as required by most credentialing organizations). Mental health professionals should assume nothing in this regard, but rather have each client educate them about what role religion plays in their life, in helping them deal with their illness, or in initiating, worsening or maintaining the illness.

If the therapist is uncomfortable asking about religious issues (i.e., taking a spiritual history) then such resistance must be overcome with training and practice. Learning about the role that religion plays in the Muslim client's illness, particularly when it influences just about everything in that person's psychological, behavioral, social, and work life, is quickly becoming the standard of care. Again, this does not mean the therapist needs to integrate those religious beliefs into the treatment, but knowing about them will be essential in providing therapy that is sensitive to and respectful of those beliefs.

2. **Provide a Safe Place**

Provide an open and safe place where clients can talk freely about their religious faith, good or bad, without judgment. Maintain a respectful, interested, and receptive attitude at all times with regard to the client's Islamic beliefs and practices (whether the person is currently active in their faith tradition or not, whether he or she speaks well of their faith or not).

3. **Anxiety**

Be alert for feelings of anxiety or excessive guilt over real or imagined sins, which Muslims may be at risk for (see Case #1 above). Don't try to immediately rationalize or explain away the anxiety/guilt; rather, seek to understand it better from the client's perspective. Identify core beliefs that may be driving the anxiety but do so without overtly challenging religious beliefs.

4. **Be Supportive and Neutral**

Be respectful and supportive of the Muslim client's religious beliefs/practices that he or she finds helpful (or might find helpful in the future as a way of coping with emotional issues). However, always do so from the client's perspective. If the client is receptive and open to healthy religious practices, and these are not clearly pathological, then these may be encouraged; if the client shows any resistance, don't push. However, it may be informative to gently explore where the resistance to religious beliefs/practices is coming from in a future session. Never give clients the impression that they are not religious enough, since they probably get plenty of that from family and members of their religious community. Whether you are a psychiatrist prescribing biological therapies or a therapist providing counseling, the mental health professional should be viewed by the client as neutral, interested in, open to and supportive of the client's Islamic faith tradition, but always on the client's side and never judgmental. This advice also applies to Imams who are counseling members of their mosque. There may be some cases, as in Case #2 above, where engagement in religious activities with clients is permissible. However, even in those instances, the therapist should always provide an environment in which the client's preferences guide their actions. Always allow the client to lead in this regard.

5. Utilize Religious Resources

If the client is religious, but not a candidate for religiously-integrated therapy or does not prefer this approach, then the therapist should provide secular psychotherapy that is supportive and respectful of the client's Islamic beliefs. There may be times during secular psychotherapy when the client's religious beliefs may be utilized to support changes in attitude and behavior. In-depth knowledge about those religious beliefs is usually necessary (guided by a detailed spiritual history, and preferably by consultation with knowledgeable experts).

6. Consider Religiously-Integrated Therapy

When clients prefer this approach and therapists are willing, religiously-integrated cognitive behavioral therapy (CBT) from a Muslim perspective for those with depression should be considered. There are resources that may help the therapist or Imam in this regard (a Muslim CBT manual, therapist and patient workbooks, and an introductory video, all without charge) (Center for Spirituality, Theology and Health, 2014). Religiously-integrated CBT, including that from a Muslim perspective, is an evidence-based treatment that has documented effectiveness in the treatment for depression, especially in highly religious patients (Koenig et al., 2015).

7. Challenge/Re-Educate

If the client's Islamic beliefs or practices are contributing to their psychopathology, and this is confirmed following consultation with an expert from the client's local religious congregation (usually their Imam), then the following approach is suggested. First and foremost, the mental health professional should further inquire about the role that religious beliefs are playing in supporting psychopathology. The therapist should listen respectfully, gathering as much information as possible about the natural history of how religion became intertwined with the emotional problem. This must be done in an open and receptive manner and without confrontation (at least during this initial information gathering stage). There will come a time, once the therapeutic relationship is firmly established and the client feels safe and accepted, when gradual, gentle, and persistent "Socratic questioning" may help to guide the client towards a "healthier" use of their Islamic beliefs/practices. We emphasize *gradual, gentle, and persistent questioning* within an atmosphere that is safe and comfortable. Arguments over religious beliefs will almost always be unsuccessful and will adversely affect the therapeutic alliance.

8. **Consult or Refer**

When addressing religion or integrating it into the treatment seems indicated in a Muslim client, and the therapist lacks the desire or experience to do so, consideration should be given to consulting with, referring to, or conducting co-therapy with an imam, Muslim chaplain, or Muslim pastoral counselor (AMC, 2016). If clergy trained to provide counseling from a Muslim perspective are not available, then the therapist should consider obtaining additional training and experience in this regard (see Center for Spirituality, Theology and Health, 2014).

9. **Non-Religious Muslims**

If the client is not actively religious, then the mental health professional should proceed with secular psychotherapy that is respectful of their personal and cultural beliefs. Aggressive attempts to reconnect the person to his/her Islamic faith tradition should be avoided. If the client was once religious and has now become socially isolated or is despairing for lack of meaning in life, the therapist might gently ask if the client has considered re-establishing connections with their local faith community (or locate a different one). The therapist may help the client weigh the pluses and minuses of such re-involvement, but again always following the client's lead.

10. **Other Recommendations**. Finally, for therapists who see Muslim clients on a regular basis, there are several ways to make them feel welcome. Consider providing a prayer rug in the waiting room (or have a special room for this activity), a sign on the wall that indicates the direction to Mecca, and a copy of the Qur'an readily available.

Conclusions

Based on the research, our clinical experience treating Muslim clients, and common sense logic, we make a number of recommendations for mental health professionals and clergy that will assist them in providing whole person care to Muslims. We emphasize here the importance of taking a detailed spiritual history to learn about the beliefs, practices, and values of each individual person, providing a safe place where they can talk about their Muslim beliefs without judgement, showing respect and honor at all times for those beliefs, and sometimes, re-educating and challenging clients when they misunderstand Islamic teachings (but only if therapist is fully informed and does so in the gentlest and most supportive fashion).

CHAPTER 9

OVERCOMING BARRIERS TO MENTAL HEALTH CARE

Devout Muslims believe that the source of all healing is God, whether the illness is mental or physical. God is believed to be the ultimate cause of illness (as a test of faith) and its cure (because God is merciful): "When I fall sick, God restores me to health...He who cures me when I am ill; He who will make me die and then give me life again" (26:80-82). When Muslims follow these verses from the Qur'an, completely trusting in God and resigning to his will, they believe that healing will take place. As science has repeatedly shown (Benson, 2009), belief can be a powerful healer, and as noted above, Muslims believe that nothing happens apart from God's will.

How does this belief in "God's will" relate to seeking and receiving conventional mental health care? Fazlur Rahman (1998) refers to a statement from a conservative Islamic theologian in the 9th century saying, "Medical treatment is permissible, but its abandonment is better" (p 48). Rahman then tells the story of a conversation between a Sufi saint and a friend when the former was sick (whether the sickness was physical or mental is unknown). Her friend (Sufyani) said to the Sufi saint: "If you pray to God he will ease your suffering." She replied, "O Sufyani! Do you not know who has willed my suffering? Is it not God?" Sufyani replied, "Yes." The Sufi then said, "If you know this, why do you ask me to pray for what contradicts His will?" (p 49). Thus, yes indeed, strong belief in God's will may reduce the likelihood that a Muslim with emotional problems will seek secular mental health care and comply with it (Lipson & Meleis, 1983; Walpole et al., 2013).

However, as in the case vignettes described in the last chapter, mental health professionals may draw on Islamic teachings when treating Muslim clients that provides a compromise between strictly relying on God's will and seeking conventional mental health treatments. Providing the following information may help the client in this regard. According to Muslim belief, the art of medicine is thought to have come from the prophet Idris (Rahman, 1998, p 38-39). Idris is Arabic for Enoch, who was the great-grandson of Adam through Seth and was the great-grandfather of Noah. Thus, there is a deep tradition within Islam that shows great respect for the medical arts. Likewise, a widely known Hadith reports that the Prophet Muhammad said "[Valid or beneficial] knowledge is only of two kinds: knowledge of faith and knowledge of the body" (Al-Azraq, 2006, p 3). Knowledge of the body includes scientific discoveries of treatments that influence bodily functions including the brain and nervous system.

In a 14th century Islamic manuscript entitled *Prophetic Medicine*, Al-Dhahabi (historian, biographer, and foremost authority in the canonical readings of the Qur'an) says: "…an expert doctor first tries his best by way of treatment and then puts his trust in God for his success," illustrating this with a story about how a farmer plants his seed and then trusts in God to make it grow (Rahman, 1998, p 49). The same point is made by a famous Hadith: "Anas ibn Malik reported: A man said, 'O Messenger of Allah, should I tie my camel and trust in Allah, or should I leave her untied and trust in Allah?' The Messenger of Allah, peace and blessings be upon him, said, 'Tie her and trust in Allah'" (Sunan At-Tirmidhi, #2517). The lesson here is that one should first obtain medical or psychiatric care for illness and then trust God to heal, since God may choose to heal through medication or even psychotherapy. Finally, medical historian Husain Nagamia (chairman of the International Institute of Islamic Medicine and chief of the division of cardiovascular and thoracic surgery at Tampa General Hospital, Florida), said: "Thus, in Islam disease is not looked upon as a curse from God to be endured and suffered but as an affliction for which a cure has to be sought and administered, with patience and perseverance" (Nagamia, n.d., p 1).

Based on widely-acknowledged sayings by experts from the Islamic tradition, Muslim clients can be encouraged to seek medical treatment or psychotherapy without reservation when they are sick with mental health problems. Indeed, the Prophet Muhammad advised people to seek medical attention when necessary (Farooqi, 1998; Al Dhahabi, 1961, p 103) and almost certainly did so himself (Robson, 1975, p 325). At a minimum, inquiring about and showing respect for a Muslim client's beliefs will certainly help to strengthen the therapeutic alliance, which may be as important for success (if not more so) than the particular medical or psychotherapeutic treatment that is offered (Horvath, 2001; Norcross & Hill, 2004). It may also increase compliance with that treatment (Weber & Pargament, 2014).

Conclusions

Muslims may at times be reluctant to seek formal mental health care, even though mental health problems may threaten not only their quality of life but also life itself (when there is a risk of suicide). Rather than seek assistance from mental health professionals who are trained to help them address the problems they are facing, Muslims may instead see traditional healers or depend entirely on "God's will." Islam teaches that while God's will is first and primary, God's will does not always mean that Muslims should suffer. In fact, seeking assistance in relief of suffering from trained experts may also be God's will, since this may enable the person to be more effective in serving God and doing good on the earth. If the Prophet Muhammad sought professional help when he needed it, then this is a good reason for Muslims to do likewise.

CHAPTER 10

SUMMARY AND CONCLUSIONS

Throughout this book we have tried to objectively present and even-handedly discuss many issues related to religion that are highly sensitive in the Muslim world. We make no attempt to judge a religion here, but simply examine and compare what has been discovered from systematic research studies, while interpreting these findings from different perspectives.

    Religious beliefs, practices, and values are central to how most Muslims organize and live their lives, and will invariably influence their mental health in one way or another. Self-esteem is very important to Muslims, and living according to Islamic teachings can enhance self-esteem since those teachings stress the equality of all humans, the important role that each person serves, and that second chances are available to everyone. Knowing about these connections is essential for mental health professionals who provide whole person care to Muslim clients. There are many sayings in the Qur'an (considered to be the Word of God) and Hadith (sayings of the Prophet Muhammad) that relate to mental health and may either enhance mental health or increase symptoms of illness if not understood and interpreted correctly.

Most of the research systematically reviewed in this book suggests that Muslims have similar overall mental health compared to those affiliated with other religious traditions or no affiliation, particularly when socioeconomic and environmental factors are taken into account. Furthermore, research shows that greater religiosity in Muslims is related to less depression, less anxiety, lower suicide, less substance use/abuse, greater well-being (in most studies), and helps those with severe chronic mental illness cope better with psychotic symptoms. All nine randomized clinical trials (100%) show that religiously-integrated interventions in Muslims result in greater reduction in depression and anxiety symptoms compared to conventional secular treatments or control conditions.

There is no question that the beliefs, practices, and values of this religion have tremendous power to produce hope and healing. At the same time, the misunderstanding of Islamic beliefs and teachings may also adversely affect mental health in various ways. While the Qur'an and Hadith provide a high bar for Muslims to live up to, this religion teaches that there are no perfect humans and that mistakes will invariably be made. The God of Islam is tremendously merciful and strives to forgive his people when they make mistakes. However, Muslims believe that God also wants them to learn from their mistakes and not keep repeating them. Islam teaches that only by following the Divine will and doing good in this world can Muslims live full, complete, and meaningful lives, both in this world and the next.

Given the importance of religion to most Muslims and its relationship to mental health, we made a number of suggestions for treating Muslim clients that mental health professionals should consider. These include taking a detailed spiritual history, providing an environment that is welcoming to Muslim clients, educating them about what early Islamic scholars have said about the seeking of health care, and in some cases, utilizing religious beliefs as a resource for healing by integrating them into therapy. Because of the powerful effects that Islamic beliefs and teachings can have on enhancing mental health and self-esteem, their misunderstanding can have the opposite effect. Therapists may be called on to help Muslim clients work through some of those misunderstandings, and resources on how to accomplish that have been provided here.

REFERENCES

Abdel Haleem MAS (translator) (2004). *The Qur'an*. NY, NY: Oxford World's Classics

Abdel-Khalek AM (2003). Death anxiety in Spain and five Arab countries. *Psychological Reports* 93:527-528

Abdel-Khalek AM, Lester D (2010). Constructions of religiosity, subjective well-being, anxiety, and depression in two cultures: Kuwait and USA. *International Journal of Social Psychiatry* 58(2):138-145

Abdel-Khalek AM, Tomas-Sabado J (2005). Anxiety and death anxiety in Egyptian and Spanish nursing students. *Death Studies* 29:157-169

Abu-Ras, W., & Abu-Bader, S. H. (2009). Risk factors for depression and posttraumatic stress disorder (PTSD): The case of Arab and Muslim Americans post-9/11. *Journal of Immigrant & Refugee Studies*, 7(4), 393-418.

Acevedo, G. A. (2008). Islamic fatalism and the clash of civilizations: An appraisal of a contentious and dubious theory. *Social Forces*, 86(4), 1711-1752.

AHDR (2016). *Arab Human Development Report (AHDR) 2016: Youth and the Prospects for Human Development in a Changing Reality*. United Nations Development Programme. Retrieved from http://hdr.undp.org/en/content/arab-human-development-report-2016-youth-and-prospects-human-development-changing-reality (accessed on 12/30/16)

Ahmad, S., Owoyemi, M. Y. (2012). The concept of Islamic work ethic: An analysis of some salient points in the prophetic tradition. *International Journal of Business and Social Science*, 3(20): 116-123

Al Dhahabi MBA (1961). *Al-Tibb Al-Nabawi*. Cairo, Egypt: al-Mustafa al-Bäbi al-Halabi

Al-Azraq, I. (2006). *Tashil al-Manafi' fi al-Tibb wa-al-Hikma* (Tashil). Beirut: Dar Sader Publications

Al-Hilali MT, Khan MM (translators) (1996). *The Noble Qur'an*. Riyadh, Saudi Arabia: Darussalam Publishers

AMC (2016). Association of Muslim Chaplains. Retrieved from http://associationofmuslimchaplains.com/ (last accessed 12-31-16)

Amer, M. M., & Hovey, J. D. (2012). Anxiety and depression in a post-September 11 sample of Arabs in the USA. *Social Psychiatry and Psychiatric Epidemiology*, *47*(3), 409-418.

Amr M, El-Mogy A, El-Masry R (2013). Adherence in Egyptian patients with schizophrenia: the role of insight, medication beliefs and spirituality. *Arab Journal of Psychiatry* 24 (1):60-68

Atallah SF, El-Dosoky Ar, Coker EM, Nabil KM, El-Islam MF (2001). A 22-year retrospective analysis of the changing freuqency and patterns of religious symptoms among inpatients with psychotic illness in Egypt. *Social Psychiatry and Psychiatric Epidemiology* 36:407-415

Awas, M., Kebede, D., & Alem, A. (1999). Major mental disorders in Butajira, southern Ethiopia. *Acta Psychiatrica Scandinavica*, *100*(S397), 56-64.

Azam M (2003). Al-Qaeda: the misunderstood Wahhabi connection and the ideology of violence. *The Royal Institute of International Affairs*, Middle East Programme, Briefing Paper, No. 1. Retrieved from https://www.chathamhouse.org/sites/files/chathamhouse/public/Research/International%20Security/azzaml.pdf (accessed on 12/30/16)

Azhar MZ, Varma SL, Hakim HR (1995). Phenomenological differences of delusions between schizophrenic patients of two cultures of Malaysia. *Singapore Medical Journal* 36:273-275

Azhar, M. Z., & Varma, SL (1995a). Religious psychotherapy in depressive patients. *Psychotherapy & Psychosomatics*, 63, 165-173

Azhar, M. Z., & Varma, SL (1995b). Religious psychotherapy as management of bereavement. *Acta Psychiatrica Scandinavica*, 91,233-235

Azhar, M.Z., Varma, S.L., & Dharap, A.S. (1994). Religious psychotherapy in anxiety disorder patients. *Acta Psychiatrica Scandinavica*, 90, 1-3.

Babamohamadi H, Sotodehasl N, Koenig HG, Al-Zaben F, Jahani C, Ghorbani R (2016). The effect of Holy Qur'an recitation on depressive symptoms in hemodialysis patients: A randomized clinical trial. *Journal of Religion and Health*, July 8, E-pub ahead of press

BabaMuhammadi H, Sotodehasl N, Koenig HG, Jahani C, Ghorbani R (2015). The effect of Qur'an recitation on anxiety in hemodialysis patients: A randomized clinical trial. *Journal of Religion and Health* 54(5):1921-1930

BBC (2009). Sanctity of life: Islamic teachings on abortion. British Broadcasting Corporation Retrieved from http://www.bbc.co.uk/religion/religions/islam/islamethics/abortion_1.shtml (accessed 3-13-17).

Bener, A., Abou-Saleh, M. T., Dafeeah, E. E., & Bhugra, D. (2015). The prevalence and burden of psychiatric disorders in primary health care visits in Qatar: too little time? *Journal of Family Medicine and Primary Care*, 4(1), 89-95.

Bennett, C (2008). *Understanding Christian-Muslim Relations*. London: Continuum, p 174

Benson, H. (2009). *Timeless Healing: the Power and Biology of Belief*. New York, NY: Simon and Schuster.

Bostwick, J. M., & Pankratz, V. S. (2000). Affective disorders and suicide risk: a reexamination. *American Journal of Psychiatry*, 157(12), 1925-1932.

Bowlby J (1952). *Maternal Care and Mental Health*. Geneva, Switzerland: Monograph World Health Organization

Center for Spirituality, Theology and Health (2014). *Religious Cognitive Behavioral Therapy (Muslim version). 10-Session Treatment Manual for Depression in Clients with Chronic Physical Illness* (by Ciarrocchi JW, Schechter D, Pearce MJ, Koenig HG, Vasegh S). Durham, North Carolina: Duke University. Retrieved from http://www.spiritualityandhealth.duke.edu/index.php/religious-cbt-study/therapy-manuals (accessed on 12/31/16)

Center for Spirituality, Theology and Health (2017). Crossroads (Center for Spirituality, Theology and Health newsletter that provides research updates 2010-2017). Durham, NC: Duke University. Retrieved from https://spiritualityandhealth.duke.edu/index.php/publications/crossroads (accessed on 2/9/17)

Chamie, J. (1986). Polygyny among Arabs. *Population Studies*, *40*(1), 55-66.

Chamsi-Pasha H, Albar MA (2017). Ethical dilemmas at the end of life: Islamic perspective. *Journal of Religion and Health* 56:400-410

Conrad, R., Schilling, G., Najjar, D., Geiser, F., Sharif, M., Liedtke, R., et al. (2007). Cross-cultural comparison of explanatory models of illness in schizophrenic patients in Jordan and Germany. *Psychological Reports, 101*(2), 531-546.

Demyttenaere, K., Bruffaerts, R., Posada-Villa, J., Gasquet, I., Kovess, V., Lepine, J., ... & Polidori, G. (2004). Prevalence, severity, and unmet need for treatment of mental disorders in the World Health Organization World Mental Health Surveys. *Journal of the American Medical Association 291*(21): 2581-2590.

Eapen, V., Revesz, T., & Revesz, T. (2003). Psychosocial correlates of paediatric cancer in the United Arab Emirates. *Supportive Care in Cancer, 11*(3), 185-189.

Ellis L, Wahab EA, Ratnasingan M (2013). Religiosity and fear of death: A three-nation comparison. *Mental Health, Religion & Culture* 16(2):179-199

Emari H, Vazifehdoust H, Nikoomaram H (2017). Islam and environmental consciousness: A new scale development. *Journal of Religion and Health* 56:706-724

Esack, F. (2005). *The Qur'an: A User's Guide*. Oxford England: Oneworld Publications

Farooqi MIH (1998). *Medicinal Plants in the Traditions of Prophet Muhammad: Medicinal, Aromatic and Food Plants Mentioned in the Traditions of Prophet Muhammad (SAAS)*. Lucknow, India: Sidrah Publisher. Also, see website: http://www.irfi.org/articles/articles_251_300/medicine_of_the_prophet.htm (accessed on 12/27/16)

Friedman M, Saroglou V (2010). Religiosity, psychological acculturation to the host culture, self-esteem and depressive symptoms among stigmatized and nonstigmatized religious immigrant groups in Western Europe. *Basic and Applied Social Psychology* 32:185-195

Gal G, Goldberger N, Kabaha A, Haklai Z, Gerasisy N, Gross R, Levav I (2012). Suicidal behavior among Muslim Arabs in Israel. *Social Psychiatry & Psychiatric Epidemiology* 47:11-17

Gencoz, F., Vatan, S., Walker, R. L., & Lester, D. (2007). Hopelessness and suicidality in Turkish and American respondents. *Omega: Journal of Death and Dying, 55*(4), 311-319

Guze, S.B., Robins, E. (1970). Suicide and primary affective disorder. *British Journal of Psychiatry* 117: 437–438.

Hamdan A, Tamim H (2011). Psychosocial risk and protective fators for postparum depression in the United Arab Emirates. *Archives of Women's Mental Health* 14:124-133

Hamdy, S. F. (2009). Islam, fatalism, and medical intervention: lessons from Egypt on the cultivation of forbearance (sabr) and reliance on God (tawakkul). *Anthropological Quarterly, 82*(1), 173-196.

Hassaballah AM (1996). Definition of death, organ donation and interruption of treatment in Islam. *Nephrology, Dialysis, Transplantation* 11(6):964-965

Hassan, M. K. (1988). *Pendidikan Dan Pembangunan Bersepadu.* Kuala Lumpur: Nurin Enterprise.

Hestyanti, Y. R. (2006). Children survivors of the 2004 tsunami in Aceh, Indonesia: a study of resiliency. *Annals of the New York Academy of Sciences, 1094*, 303-307

Hodge, D. R., Zidan, T., & Husain, A. (2015). Depression among Muslims in the United States: Examining the role of discrimination and spirituality as risk and protective factors. *Social Work*, swv055 (doi: 10.1093/sw/swv055).

Horvath, A. O. (2001). The alliance. *Psychotherapy: Theory, Research, Practice, Training, 38(4)*, 365-372.

Hosain, G. M., Chatterjee, N., Ara, N., & Islam, T. (2007). Prevalence, pattern and determinants of mental disorders in rural Bangladesh. *Public Health, 121*(1), 18-24.

Hosseini M, Salehi A, Khoshknab MF, Rokofian A, Davidson PM (2013). The effect of a preoperative spiritual/religious intervention on anxiety in Shia Muslim patients undergoing coronary artery bypass graft surgery: A randomized controlled trial. *Journal of Holistic Nursing*, 31(3):164-172

Inozu M, Clark DA, Karanci AN (2012). Scrupulosity in Islam: A comparison of highly religious Turkish and Canadian samples. *Behavior Therapy* 43:190-202

ISSP (2008). *International Social Survey Program*, 2008. Dataset downloaded from the Association of Religion Data Archives, www.TheARDA.com, and were collected by Dr. Max Haller and his team at the Institut für Soziologie, Universität Graz, Austria (accessed on 11/7/16).

Kazarian, S. S. (2005). Family functioning, cultural orientation, and psychological well-being among university students in Lebanon. *Journal of Social Psychology*, 145(2), 141-152.

Khodaveirdyzadeh, R., Rahimi, R., Rahmani, A., Ghahramanian, A., Kodayari, N., & Eivazi, J. (2016). Spiritual/religious coping strategies and their relationship with illness adjustment among Iranian breast cancer patients. *Asian Pacific Journal of Cancer Prevention*, *17*(8), 4095-4099.

Koenig HG, Al Shohaib S (2014). *Health and Well-being in Islamic Societies: Background, Research, and Applications*. Cham, Switzerland: Springer International

Koenig HG, King DE, Carson VB (2012). *Handbook of Religion and Health*, 2nd ed. New York, NY: Oxford University Press

Koenig HG, Pearce MJ, Nelson B, Shaw SF, Robins CJ, Daher N, Cohen HJ, Berk LS, Bellinger D, Pargament KI, Rosmarin DH, Vasegh S, Kristeller J, Juthani N, Nies D, King MB (2015). Religious vs. conventional cognitive-behavioral therapy for major depression in persons with chronic medical illness. *Journal of Nervous and Mental Disease* 203(4):243-251

Levav I, Aiesenberg E (1989). Suicide in Israel: Cross-national comparisons. *Acta Psychiatrica Scandinavica* 79:468-473

Lin, C. C. (2015). Gratitude and depression in young adults: The mediating role of self-esteem and well-being. *Personality and Individual Differences*, *87*, 30-34.

Lipson, J. G., & Meleis, A. I. (1983). Issues in health care of Middle Eastern patients. *Western Journal of Medicine*, *139*(6), 854-861.

McClellan, M. (2012). Abraham and the chronology of ancient Mesopotamia. *Answers Research Journal* 5:141–150.

Mokdad, A. H., Jaber, S., Aziz, M. I. A., Al Buhairan, F., Al Ghaithi, A., Al Hamad, N. M., ... & Al Sowaidi, S. (2014). The state of health in the Arab world, 1990–2010: an analysis of the burden of diseases, injuries, and risk factors. *The Lancet, 383*(9914), 309-320.

Moussavi, S., Chatterji, S., Verdes, E., Tandon, A., Patel, V., & Ustun, B. (2007). Depression, chronic diseases, and decrements in health: results from the World Health Surveys. *The Lancet, 370*(9590), 851-858.

Nagamia HF (n.d.). Medicine in Islam, p 1. Retrieved from http://www.iiim.org/historyhim.html (accessed on 12/27/16)

Nasr SH (2002). *The Heart of Islam*. New York, NY: HarperCollins

Ndetei DM, Muriungi SK, Owoso A, Mutiso VN, Mbwayo AW, Khasakhala LI, Barch DM, Mamah D (2012). Prevalence and characteristics of psychotic-like experiences in Kenyan youth. *Psychiatry Research* 196:235-242

Noegel SB, Wheeler BM (2003). Injil. *Historical Dictionary of Prophets in Islam and Judaism.* Lanham, MD: Scarecrow Press

Norcross JC, Hill CE (2004). Empirically supported therapy relationships. *Clinical Psychologist* 57:19-24

Nurasikin, M. S., Khatijah, L. A., Aini, A., Ramli, M., Aida, S. A., Zainal, N. Z., & Ng, C. G. (2013). Religiousness, religious coping methods and distress level among psychiatric patients in Malaysia. *International Journal of Social Psychiatry* 59(4):332-338.

Ozkan M, Altindag A, Oto R, Sentunali E (2006). Mental health aspects of Turkish women from polygamous versus monogamous families. *International Journal of Social Psychiatry* 52(3):214-220

Pew Research Center (2011). The future of the global Muslim population. *Pew Research Center: Religion & Public Life*. Retrieved from http://www.pewforum.org/2011/01/27/the-future-of-the-global-muslim-population/ (accessed on 12/24/16).

Pew Research Center (2012). *The World's Muslims: Unity and Diversity* (Chapter 1. Religious affiliation). Retrieved from http://www.pewforum.org/2012/08/09/the-worlds-muslims-unity-and-diversity-1-religious-affiliation/ (last accessed 12/24/16).

Pew Research Center (2015). The future of world religions: Population growth projections, 2010-2050. *Religion & Public Life*, April 2. Retrieved from http://www.pewforum.org/2015/04/02/religious-projections-2010-2050 (accessed on 1/30/2017)

Polanczyk, G. V., Salum, G. A., Sugaya, L. S., Caye, A., & Rohde, L. A. (2015). Annual Research Review: A meta-analysis of the worldwide prevalence of mental disorders in children and adolescents. *Journal of Child Psychology and Psychiatry*, *56*(3), 345-365.

Pritchard, C., & Amanullah, S. (2007). An analysis of suicide and undetermined deaths in 17 predominantly Islamic countries contrasted with the UK. *Psychological Medicine*, *37*(3), 421-430

Rahman F (1998). *Health and Medicine in the Islamic Tradition*. Chicago, IL: ABC International Group, Inc. (Kazi Publications)

Razali, S. M., Aminah, K., Khan, U.A. (2002). Religious-cultural psychotherapy in the management of anxiety patients. *Transcultural Psychiatry* 39 (1), 130-136

Razali, S. M., Hasanah, CI, Aminah, K., Subramaniam, M. (1998). Religious--sociocultural psychotherapy in patients with anxiety and depression. *Australian & New Zealand Journal of Psychiatry*, 32, 867-872

Rehman KL (1993): Cardio-pulmonary resuscitation and life support: The current laws and the Muslim perspective. *Journal of the Islamic Medical Association* 25: 20-22

Robson J (1975). *Mishkat Al-Masabih*. NY, NY: Orientalia Art Ltd

Saffari M, Pakpour aH, Naderi MK, Koenig HG, Baldacchino DR, Piper CN (2013). Spiritual coping, religiosity and quality of life: a stud on Muslim patients undergoing haemodialysis. *Nephrology* 18:269-275

Salib, E., & Youakim, S. (2001). Spiritual healing in elderly psychiatric patients: A case-control study in an Egyptian psychiatric hospital. *Aging & Mental Health, 5*(4), 366-370.

Sarhill N, LeGrands S, Islambouli R, Davis MP, Walsh D (2001). The terminally ill Muslim: death and dying from the Muslim perspective. *American Journal of Hospice and Palliative Care* 18(4):251-5

Scholte, W. F., Olff, M., Ventevogel, P., de Vries, G.-J., Jansveld, E., Lopes Cardozo, B., et al. (2004). Mental health symptoms following war and repression in Eastern Afghanistan. *Journal of the American Medical Association, 292*(5), 585-593.

Schwartz S (2014). Saudi Wahhabism and ISIS Wahhabism: The Difference. *Standard*, Oct 24 Retrieved from http://www.weeklystandard.com/saudi-wahhabism-and-isis-wahhabism-the-difference/article/816954 (accessed on 12/30/16).

Shah A, Chandia M (2010). The relationship between suicide and Islam: a cross-national study. *Journal of Injury & Violence Research* 2(2):93-97

Suhail, K., & Chaudhry, H. R. (2004). Predictors of subjective well-being in an Eastern Muslim culture. *Journal of Social & Clinical Psychology, 23(3), 359-376.*

Telegraph Reporters (2016). What is Wahhabism? The reactionary branch of Islam said to be 'the main source of global terrorism.' *The Telegraph*, March 29. Retrieved from http://www.telegraph.co.uk/news/2016/03/29/what-is-wahhabism-the-reactionary-branch-of-islam-said-to-be-the/ (accessed on 12/30/16).

Tomas-Sabado, J., Gomez-Benito, J. (2004). Note on death anxiety in Spain and five Arab countries. *Psychological Reports, 95*(3 Pt 2), 1239-1240.

Tondo, L., Baldessarini, R. J., Hennen, J., Minnai, G. P., Salis, P., Scamonatti, L., Masia M, Ghiani C, & Mannu, P. (1999). Suicide attempts in major affective disorder patients with comorbid substance use disorders. *Journal of Clinical Psychiatry* 60(suppl 2): 63-69.

United Nations Development Programme (2016). Arab Human Development Report 2016: Enabling youth to shape their own future key to progress on development and stability in Arab region. November 29. Retrieved from http://www.undp.org/content/undp/en/home/presscenter/pressreleases/2016/11/29/arab-human-development-report-2016-enabling-youth-to-shape-their-own-future-key-to-progress-on-development-and-stability-in-arab-region-.html (accessed on 12/30/16)

Wahass, S., Kent, G. (1997). Coping with auditory hallucinations: A cross-cultural comparison between Western (British) and non-Western (Saudi Arabian) patients. *Journal of Nervous and Mental Disease*, 185, 664-668

Walpole, S. C., McMillan, D., House, A., Cottrell, D., & Mir, G. (2013). Interventions for treating depression in Muslim patients: a systematic review. *Journal of Affective Disorders, 145*(1), 11-20.

Weber, S. R., & Pargament, K. I. (2014). The role of religion and spirituality in mental health. *Current Opinion in Psychiatry, 27*(5), 358-363.

Whiteford, H. A., Degenhardt, L., Rehm, J., Baxter, A. J., Ferrari, A. J., Erskine, H. E., ... & Burstein, R. (2013). Global burden of disease attributable to mental and substance use disorders: findings from the Global Burden of Disease Study 2010. *The Lancet, 382*(9904), 1575-1586.

Whiteford, H. A., Ferrari, A. J., Degenhardt, L., Feigin, V., & Vos, T. (2015). The global burden of mental, neurological and substance use disorders: an analysis from the global burden of disease study 2010. *PLoS One, 10*(2), e0116820.

WVS (2005-2006). *World Values Survey*, 2005-2006. Dataset was downloaded from the World Values Survey (WORLD VALUES SURVEY Wave 5 2005-2008 OFFICIAL AGGREGATE v.20140429. World Values Survey Association [www.worldvaluessurvey.org]. Aggregate File Producer: Asep/JDS, Madrid SPAIN). Retrieved from http://www.worldvaluessurvey.org/WVSDocumentationWV5.jsp (accessed on 11-7-16)

Yahya H (2010). *The Prophet Jesus (as) and Hazrat Mahdi (as) Will Come This Century*. Istanbul, Turkey: Global Publishing.

Yorulmaz, O., Gencoz, T., Woody, S. (2009). OCD cognitions and symptoms in different religious contexts. *Journal of Anxiety Disorders* 23, 401-406

ABOUT THE AUTHORS

Harold G. Koenig, M.D., M.H.Sc., completed his undergraduate education at Stanford University, nursing school at San Joaquin Delta College, medical school training at the University of California at San Francisco, and geriatric medicine, psychiatry, and biostatistics training at Duke University Medical Center. He is currently board certified in general psychiatry, and formerly boarded in family medicine, geriatric medicine, and geriatric psychiatry, and is on the faculty at Duke as Professor of Psychiatry and Behavioral Sciences, and Associate Professor of Medicine. He is also Adjunct Professor in the Department of Medicine at King Abdulaziz University, Jeddah, Saudi Arabia, and in the School of Public Health at Ningxia Medical University, Yinchuan, People's Republic of China. Dr. Koenig is Director of the Center for Spirituality, Theology and Health at Duke University Medical Center, and has over 500 scientific peer-reviewed articles and book chapters, and nearly 50 books in print or preparation. Dr. Koenig has given testimony before the U.S. Senate (1998) and U.S. House of Representatives (2008) concerning the benefits of religion and spirituality on public health, and travels widely to give seminars and workshops on this topic. He is the recipient of the 2012 Oskar Pfister Award from the American Psychiatric Association.

Saad Saleh Al Shohaib, M.D., completed his medical training at the Faculty of Medicine, King Abdulaziz University, Jeddah, Saudi Arabia. He completed a Canadian Fellowship in Medicine and a Fellowship in Nephrology at McGill University, Montréal, Canada. He is a Fellow of the American College of Physicians (FACP), and completed the American Board of General Medicine and the American Board of Nephrology. He is currently University Professor of Medicine and Nephrology at King Abdulaziz University (KAU) faculty of medicine and is a consultant nephrologist and Chief of Medical Staff at Bagedo and Erfan Hospital in Jeddah. Dr. Al Shohaib is a member of the Arab Society of Nephrology, Saudi Society of Nephrology, and is founder and ex-president of the Nephrology Cub in the Western Region of Saudi Arabia. He is the author or co-author of many academic research publications and case reports on kidney disease, dialysis, and transplantation, and is co-author of *Health and Well-Being in Islamic Societies* (2014, Springer).

Made in the USA
San Bernardino, CA
09 May 2018